The US Dollar
and
Global Hegemony

The US Dollar
and
Global Hegemony

by

Thomas Costigan
and
Drew Cottle

Vij Books India Pvt Ltd

New Delhi (India)

Published by

Vij Books India Pvt Ltd
(Publishers, Distributors & Importers)
2/19, Ansari Road
Delhi – 110 002
Phones: 91-11-43596460, 91-11-47340674
M: 9811094883
e-mail: orders@vijpublishing.com
www.vijbooks.com

ISBN: 978-81-94261-80-3 (Paperback)
ISBN: 978-81-94261-81-0 (ebook)

Acknowledgements

We gratefully acknowledge the assistance of Dr
Angela Keys in editing an earlier draft of this book.

Contents

List of Acronyms

ACPFP	Advisory Committee on Postwar Foreign Policy
AIIB	Asian Infrastructure Investment Bank
ALBA	Bolivarian Alliance for Latin America
ARAMCO	Saudi American Oil Company
BRICS	Brazil, Russia, India, China, South Africa
CASOC	California Arabian Standard Oil Company
CFR	Council on Foreign Relations
CIPS	China International Payment System
CSTO	Collective Security Treaty Organisation
GDP	Gross Domestic Product
GFC	Global Financial Crisis
IMF	International Monetary Fund
NATO	North Atlantic Treaty Organization
NIC	National Intelligence Council
OBOR	One Belt One Road
OPEC	Organisation of Petroleum Exporting Countries
SCO	Shanghai Cooperation Organization
USSR	Union of Soviet Socialist Republics

CSIS	Centre for Strategic and International Studies
WMD	Weapons of Mass Destruction
SWIFT	Society for Worldwide Interbank Financial Telecommunication
RMB	Renminbi

Introduction

In the 20th century, the creation of an informal American empire involved the establishment of a global system in which other capitalist states operated under the aegis of the United States (Panitch & Gindin, 2012, p. 8). This informal American empire, centred upon US hegemony, was conceived and planned as a "Grand Area" of US influence through the considered deliberations by the Council on Foreign Relations (CFR) in close collaboration with US State Department planners. An important account of the planning and analysis that established the Grand Area and US hegemony has been provided by Shoup and Minter's 2004 study. However, Shoup and Minter's crucial study understates the role that the US dollar plays in the functioning of US global hegemony. This book demonstrates that the US dollar is a vital medium that has made possible America's informal empire.

This book examines the political economy of the United States (US) dollar in its role as world reserve currency in the post-World War II period. It explains how the US dollar rose to prominence as the world's reserve currency and argues that the US dollar and its reserve status give the US a vast amount of hegemonic power. It analyses debates about whether the US dollar might be coming to the end of a period in which it has been the dominant reserve currency due to geopolitical factors, such as the rise of the BRICS nations – Brazil, Russia, India, China and South Africa, as well as US concerns about its spiralling level of government debt. With its national currency as the world's reserve currency, the United States has been able to exercise hegemonic power in the international sphere. Moves to diminish the US dollar's role as the world's reserve currency, including the reduction or removal of its oil-trading function, have the capacity to undermine US hegemony. This was recognised in a report by the United States National Intelligence Council (2012, p. xii) which stated that:

> ... the fall of the dollar as the global reserve currency and substitution by another or a basket of currencies would be one of the sharpest indications of a loss of US global economic position, strongly undermining Washington's political influence too.

The US dollar is at the core of the global financial system and its reserve currency status has enabled US hegemony to function through an integrated world economy, serving US economic interests in accordance with the "Grand Area policy" (Hossain-Zadeh, 2006).

This book comprises five chapters and analyses the period from the late 19th century until 2016. During this period, the changing global conditions and contexts enabled the US to develop and exercise global economic hegemony.

Chapter One examines the reproduction of US laws and financial structures in Latin America in the late 19th century. The chapter also considers the currency crisis of the 1930s, where the British Sterling Area experienced crisis while the importance of the United States dollar as a source of liquidity increased. The build-up to World War II is explored in Chapter 1, demonstrating that the Roosevelt administration viewed certain global events as threats, such as Japan's invasion of China and its potential expansion into South Asia, as well as Germany's encroachment upon its neighbours. The Roosevelt administration began to consider how these events would affect the position of the United States.

Chapter Two details the hegemonic intent of the actions undertaken by the Roosevelt administration. It examines events from 1937 to 1945 and demonstrates the planning that enabled the construction of a United States-centric world system. Planners in the State Department and the Council on Foreign Relations (CFR) formulated the "Grand Area" concept. This chapter demonstrates how the US dollar came to be of vital importance and argues that it is the medium that binds disparate areas of the world together under United States hegemony. The creation of international institutions such as the International Monetary Fund (IMF) and the World Bank are also explored in this chapter.

Chapter Three examines the emergence of US global hegemony between 1955 and 1974 through the use of the US dollar as the world's reserve currency. In Chapter Three, the incident of the 1956 Suez Crisis illustrates how the US used economic pressure to force the British to leave Egypt through its financial hegemony. This chapter also explains how US hegemony began to decline within a period of twenty years because of the debts incurred through President Johnson's Great Society reforms. The context of the Cold War, combined with the escalating costs of the American War in Vietnam, demonstrated what is known as the "Triffin Dilemma". The economist, Robert Triffin, had identified a dilemma involving the US dollar's function as the world reserve currency and its simultaneous domestic function within the US. The dilemma concerned the balance of payments crisis that would arise from a conflict between the domestic and international functions of the US dollar. Chapter Three also considers the crucial decision by the Nixon administration to abandon the gold standard and the agreement that Saudi Arabian oil would be paid for exclusively in US dollars, an agreement that still continues.

Chapter Four analyses the US dollar and geopolitical events from 1974 to the 2008 Global Financial Crisis (GFC) and its aftermath. This chapter gives a detailed explanation of how the United States went from being the biggest creditor in the world to the biggest debtor during the Reagan administration, thus threatening the long-term sustainability of United States finances.

Chapter Four demonstrates that the combined effect of changes in the world system, such as the economic rise of China, may represent a terminal threat to the United States as a hegemonic power, with a decline in the conditions that had once allowed US hegemony to flourish.

Chapter Five examines key events in the period after the 2008 Global Financial Crisis. This chapter analyses the debate about the US dollar's role as the world's reserve currency, and whether this role will endure. The chapter evaluates the arguments for and against the continuation of the US dollar as the global reserve currency.

The Conclusion highlights the ongoing problem of the balance of payments deficits between the US and the rest of the world, which has been an issue for over one hundred years.

CHAPTER ONE

Pre-War US Capitalism

Pre-1939

This chapter examines how the US dollar became an important source of international liquidity in the interwar years. Prior to the Bretton Woods conference of 1944, the US dollar and the US financial system more broadly were already playing a vital role in world finance. The United States emerged from World War I in a powerful political and economic position, but due to domestic conflicts, it did not exercise its newfound power. Several overarching features marked the pre-World War II period. Western capitalist power had been slowly shifting from Britain to the United States. The Gross Domestic Product (GDP) of the United States had overtaken that of Britain in the 1870s and the dollar was becoming increasingly important as a source of liquidity to Europe, given that many European nations, particularly Britain, were experiencing debt and deficit problems associated with the costs of World War I. In addition, there was no clear hegemon to regulate world affairs, or the economic and political matters of the Western capitalist world.

The purpose of this chapter is to demonstrate how US capitalism, and more specifically the US dollar, emerged from its continental isolation to play a critical role in world finance. To achieve this, the chapter examines how the internationalisation of the US state proceeded from the late 19th century and extended up to and beyond World War II, when the relationship of the US to the rest of the world took on a markedly wider scope in practice and conception. From the late 19th century American capitalism began to take on a more internationalist outlook and sought out new markets and investments across the globe. This transformation required giving primacy to the property rights of private investors, and the establishment of suitable political administrations (Reinsch, 1902). This expansion became critical to America's economic relations with the Caribbean and Latin America. Panitch and Gindin (2012, p. 41) argue that this transformation required the US to adopt a policing role to superimpose on other nations the policies necessary to guarantee the property rights of private investors outside US borders.

Several important changes occurred in how the United States expanded its influence overseas. The Open Door policy, the establishment of the Federal Reserve Board in 1913, and the gold standard were instrumental to the growing consolidation and confidence of US capitalism. The United States' victory against Spain in the 1898 Spanish-American War cemented US control over much of the Caribbean and the Pacific. This was combined with the reproduction of the American state's legal, administrative and political methods of control. These changes were designed to facilitate the dominance of private capital beyond the borders of the United States, and they demonstrated how the dollar was becoming increasingly internationalised. United States government support for regimes that were less than liberal, in contrast to the stated liberal world order it was pursuing, show that the motive was the reproduction of United States capitalism abroad(Schmitz, 1999). What began to emerge from this expansion is what Panitch and Gindin (2012) term an "informal empire". The world was increasingly being divided into spheres of influence and the Western powers competed for control of markets and resources. In the pre-World War II period, the world had still not been subsumed under a single capitalist power that was able to regulate a new world system.

This chapter explains the importance of the role that the US dollar played in financing European war expenditure during World War I. Through this role, the dollar was becoming an ever more important source of liquidity in the world economy. However, unlike the situation after World War II, the US did not develop a coherent geo-strategic worldview or conception of its place or function in the world system, preferring to concentrate on domestic matters. However, during the presidency of Woodrow Wilson, there was a very strong drive to continue the expansion of American industry and finance. The diplomatic negotiations between the United States and other powers, particularly Britain, are examined in this chapter, which also focuses on increasing US concern about aggression in Europe and Asia which led to World War II.

The Internationalisation of US Capitalism

The United States victory in the brief Spanish-American War cemented US dominance over important geo-strategic spheres essential to the US economy and US security. The victory also provided the US with a launch pad into Asia, particularly China. In 1898 the Treaty of Paris was signed to officially end hostilities. The Treaty required Spain to cede control of Guam, Puerto Rico and the Philippines to the United States, thereby expanding US influence across the Pacific. The Treaty also guaranteed the independence of Cuba from Spain. During the conflict, the United States annexed Hawaii, and through an act of Congress, Hawaii officially became US territory on 12 August 1898. From this victory, the United States emerged as a power in the Pacific. The importance of the victory in strategic terms allowed the United States to create a large sphere of influence with the ability to project economic and military power into Latin America and Asia ('The Spanish-American War, 1898', n.d.).

Growing US influence in the Pacific after its victory over Spain saw the US adopt an Open Door Policy towards China. With Spanish influence in the Pacific vastly reduced, the US sphere of influence reached all the way to into East Asia. The Open Door Policy was intended to secure international consensus on the trading rights of foreign nations operating in China. China experts Alfred E. Hippisley and William W. Rockhill proposed an open trading policy for foreign nations doing business in China. With advice from Hippisley and Rockhill, on 6 September 1899 Secretary of State Hay sent the first of the Open Door Notes to the other great powers operating in China – Britain, France, Russia, Germany and Japan. The Notes proposed free and open access for trade, and respect for spheres of influence established in China by the great powers. Hay believed that benefits would accrue to American traders in China by harmonising access to that country and helping to mitigate disputes. The policy largely aimed to secure American interests in China through a mutually beneficial diplomatic agreement with the Chinese ('Secretary of State John Hay and the Open Door in China, 1899–1900', n.d.).

A critical moment for the dollar occurred in 1913 with the US Federal Reserve Act. The United States Federal Reserve played a crucial role in internationalising the dollar. The Act was the culmination of a long process aimed at greater regulation and currency stabilisation in the United States dating back to the mid-19th century. The 1907 financial shock demonstrated that the US financial system was unable to deal with the instability created by uncontrolled competition between increasingly large banking cartels. Prior to World War I, New York had surpassed London as a major source of liquidity and the United States had far surpassed Britain in industrial output (Panitch &Gindin, 2012, p. 42). By this time the US financial system had become so large that a "bankers' bank" was needed to mitigate the financial crisis. This was achieved by melding government and Wall Street together to protect and promote US capital, by giving investors the confidence in the backing of the US government. With the ability of private finance, led by J.P. Morgan, to have their credit guaranteed by the Federal Reserve, these private financiers had succeeded in taking control of the US money supply (Engdahl, 2011, p. 44).

With the power of private capitalists and their close institutional association with the US government, the US dollar could proceed to spread into Europe as a critical source of liquidity to both governments and private firms alike. In this way, as the US dollar was internationalised, so too was the American state (Panitch & Gindin, 2012, p. 43). The gold standard played an important role in the history of US finance. Until 1971, the US was on either a bi-metallic standard throughout the 19th century, or a singular gold standard that existed until 1971. The gold standard functioned as a geo-strategic confidence builder in the US dollar, and it had the effect of bringing nations that adopted it into the economic orbit of the US.

The gold standard and its relationship to US geo-strategy in the context of expanding US trade in Latin America was crucial and it came to be referred to as "dollar diplomacy" (Rosenberg, 1985). From 1900 to 1915, US policy makers sought ways to stabilise trade and bring confidence to investors in Latin America. The use of the US dollar as a national currency for Latin American nations was openly advocated. Economists, led by Charles Contant, believed that the use of the dollar in the region would help bring "progress and modernisation" to the region (Helleiner, 2003). This would be achieved by US trading partners in Latin America depositing their gold in the US and denominating their holdings in US dollars. With this arrangement in place the US could begin to "dollarize" the region.

An example of this arrangement at work can be found in Puerto Rico. Puerto Rico was the first jurisdiction where the US attempted to encourage a gold standard. The adoption of the US dollar and gold standard for Puerto Rico was a straightforward process, with important business interests supportive of the move which would make accessing the US much easier. By 1933 the gold standard had come to an end. After the Great Depression, which began in 1929 and lasted for more than a decade, the US government, as well as the nation's financial institutions, required a much more liquid financial system. A gold standard has the effect of restricting the issuance of capital by tying it to the amount and valuation of gold (Elwell, 2012). When President Roosevelt came to office in March 1933 he took a series of drastic measures to end the gold standard and supply capital markets with liquidity. The convertibility of gold was abolished and private gold holdings were nationalised. Roosevelt declared a bank holiday lasting from 6 March 1933 to 9 March 1933, preventing withdrawals of privately held gold (Roots, 2000).

World War I

World War I was a conflagration that consumed the empires of European nations. But while the history of World War I battles is well known and studied, the simultaneous battle that was being waged by diplomats, politicians and business people is less well understood. Amongst allied and enemy nations, negotiations over how to fund the war effort were fraught with tension and subterfuge. Debt became a defining feature of the war for all participants and would be one of the War's strongest legacies (Hudson, 2003, p. 39). The interwar years were also remarkable for the number and seriousness of the economic and political crises that gripped both Britain and the United States, the most notable of these being the start of the Great Depression (1929) and the sterling crisis of 1931.

World War I and the interwar years which followed it marked a turning point in the trajectory of Western hegemony. Britain had been the major hegemon in the world system for approximately two centuries. However, with the British Empire in decline and the emergence of new strategic competitors, the world system was entering an era of profound instability. During the period from approximately 1914 to 1939, no nation possessed the full array of strategic resources necessary to dominate the world and establish a new political order. The United States did have at its disposal massive industrial, economic and financial power; however, it lacked a clear strategic conception of its role in the world during the interwar years. The Grand Area policy drawn up during World War II is a stark contrast to the ad hoc nature of US diplomacy and military strategy during the interwar years.

The British war effort in World War I was largely dependent on material and financial support from the United States. This dependence reflected new political realities for Britain. By World War I, Britain and the United States had become near equals in the economic sphere. World War I further aggravated the economic difficulties that Britain was experiencing, forcing the government to sell assets to pay for the war. The United States was able to supply to Britain all of the war materials and economic assistance that it required. This is symbolic of the changing fortunes of Britain, and the fact that it was so heavily reliant on the United States demonstrated the new distribution of world power. After World War I the United States became an important creditor for the world (Lake, 2000). In the post-World War I period, financial power shifted from London to New York.

At the same time, the United States began to practice a more interventionist approach in protecting private US investments. President Woodrow Wilson's worldview and economic outlook greatly expanded the international scope of US hegemony. The US took on the characteristics of an empire by making links between the economic and commercial concerns of private enterprise and the geo-strategy necessary to ensure these interests remained in US hands. Schmitz (1999) argues that the US claims to be committed to liberal democracy and human rights, but more pragmatic policy objectives cause the US to support right-wing autocrats who are ideologically more acceptable to US capital than populist and leftist regimes. Schmitz states that this approach has since come to be institutionalised in the formulation of US foreign policy. Beginning his study in 1921, Schmitz argues that the administration of Woodrow Wilson played a critical role in determining the way that US policy towards foreign nations was shaped, particularly about the role played by US investments. Wilson's approach was to initiate policies that were conducive to US investments (Schmitz, 1999). Panitch and Gindin (2012) also argue that it was the administration of Woodrow Wilson which saw the US taking a more keen interest in how foreign nations related to US commercial interests.

US Diplomacy Leads

The formation of post-war policy in the Roosevelt administration is intertwined with the personal relationships and world views of the individuals involved. One of the most crucial of these individuals was Under Secretary of State Sumner Welles. Welles played a decisive role in the formation and direction of policy in the Roosevelt administration. Welles came to work in the State Department at a time when it was in virtual crisis due to the departure of Bill Phillips in 1937. Roosevelt was well acquainted with Welles, and had provided him with a reference to join the US Foreign Service in 1916. Welles had enjoyed a successful diplomatic career long before his work on post-war planning. In 1920 aged 28, Welles became the Chief of Latin American Affairs Division in the State Department and was considered an authority on the region. He later informed the "good neighbour policy" (Rofe, 2007). Welles had direct access to Roosevelt in the White House. Welles' vision of United States diplomacy and how post-war policy should be structured was influenced by another American President: Woodrow Wilson. Harper (1994, p. 60) explains that:

> Welles' diplomacy was inspired in part by Wilson's "peace without victory" formula of 1917—by the hope of bringing American leverage to bear during the military stalemate in order to settle European matters definitively and in a manner favourable to the United States.

Similarly, O'Sullivan (1999) argues that Welles used the post-war planning opportunity that Roosevelt had initiated to put into practice his own views on what role the United States should take after the war. He viewed his "leadership of post war planning as an opportunity to realize his neo-Wilsonian vision of a world reordered along lines desired by the United States" (O'Sullivan, 1999).

The American population in the late 1930s held predominantly isolationist views (Welles, 1997). It was in this context that the Roosevelt administration tried to avoid war with Japan. With isolationist sentiment in the US growing, Roosevelt delivered his "Quarantine" speech in October 1937 in Chicago, the heartland of isolationism in the United States (Borg, 1957). This speech contained much of the thinking and planning that the Roosevelt administration had done regarding Japanese expansion in the Pacific. The word "quarantine" is indicative of the global outlook that the Roosevelt administration was increasingly taking as it responded to the movements of the Japanese in Asia, and Germany in Europe.

Sumner Welles was described as "FDR's global planner" due to the increasingly global scope of Welles' diplomatic and planning work in the late-1930s, which was conducted in the context of a world that was quickly spiralling towards war (Welles, 1997, p. 205). After Roosevelt's "Quarantine" speech in October 1937, Welles formulated a two pronged plan and submitted it to Roosevelt in December 1937. The plan was designed to use the influence of the United States to assure allies and enemies alike that the United States would not remain uninvolved in world affairs. The plan avoided making any direct military commitments by the United States. The tactics of this plan were twofold. The United States would offer to cut tariffs, cooperate on disarmament and give greater access to raw materials to other nations. The second phase of the plan involved creating an "executive committee". It was intended that nine nations from Latin America as well as Europe and Asia would join this committee with the intention of organising an international contingent of nations, centred upon the United States, aimed at preventing war (Welles, 1997).

It is important to note here that United States' planning was based on two priorities. The first was to restrict Japan's sphere of influence and ability to operate militarily in Asia. The second priority up until 1939 was to prevent war by offering inducements to other nations not to go to war as per Welles's plan of 1937. With this policy the United States was beginning to think in global terms about its security and economic situation. As a major international actor, the United States was part of a newly emerging world order in which it would increasingly play a fundamental role. The consideration of world events far away from the continental United States, and how these events would impact United States' interests, became the foundation for later hegemonic policies that Sumner Welles would advance during the Second World War.

Although the US State Department took the lead in foreign relations and government planning, the Treasury Department also played a crucial role in United States' post-war policy and in cementing the US dollar's global hegemony. Henry Morgenthau Jr. led the Treasury Department. He became Secretary of the Treasury in 1933, replacing William Wooden who had fallen ill. As Morgenthau was of Jewish descent, he was vocal in his opposition to Nazi Germany and began to use his new role to combat the Nazi regime. He did this by imposing tariffs on German imports under the Smoot Hawley Tariff Act. However, this led to friction with the US State Department, which still wanted to maintain a reasonably friendly relationship with Hitler's government, fearing a loss of trade, which by 1940 represented US$206 million in the German automotive sector, up from US$151 million in 1936 (Offner, 1977). Morgenthau had called the State Department approach "timorous and conventional, dominated by the foreign office notion that you get things done by being a generous host at diplomatic banquets" (Blum, 1959). However, Morgenthau did respect Sumner Welles's contribution to the foreign policy of the United States. As Secretary of the Treasury, Morgenthau was responsible for foreign monetary policy. This responsibility made Morgenthau a central figure in post-war planning and the construction of United States hegemony.

In 1937, Morgenthau grew increasingly concerned about the prospect of war in Europe and the advances of Japan in Asia. According to Blum (1959), Morgenthau feared the spread of fascism as a threat to the liberal democratic ideals that he held dear. Blum posits that in his capacity as Treasury Secretary in the Roosevelt administration, Morgenthau was not in a strong position to act to prevent war or combat totalitarianism, however fervently he may have believed in the need to do so. However, this interpretation is challenged by Offner (1977) who argues that Morgenthau in his official capacity did what he could to resist Hitler, although in retrospect minor tariffs on German exports from one sector would not have been sufficient to disrupt German activity.

In 1937 two critical issues faced the Roosevelt administration and Morgenthau was directly involved in the administration's efforts to resolve them. The first of these issues was the Japanese invasion of north China and the second was the recession of 1937–38. The Roosevelt administration found that in the late 1930s it had little ability to respond to Japanese advances. Adams (1971) and Blum (1959) make apparent the lack of a clear policy on the part of the Roosevelt administration to deal with Japanese aggression. The attacks on Pearl Harbor catalysed US policy. The Japanese invasion of China confronted the Roosevelt administration with a strategic dilemma. Adams (1971) argues that this dilemma concerned how United States investments and the lives of Americans in China would be affected by Japanese occupation. While the Roosevelt administration did not approve of the invasion, it was not prepared to act militarily to stop it.

A press conference by US Secretary of State, Cordell Hull, on 16 July 1937 revealed the perspective of United States officials on the prominent role they believed the United States should take in world affairs. Hull announced that "the existence of serious hostilities anywhere in the world affected the interests, rights, and obligations of the United States" (Adams, 1971). The Roosevelt administration imposed an embargo against Japan after it invaded China on July 1937. The embargo was intended to pressure the Japanese to halt their advance into China. With the Japanese heavily dependent on American and British markets, it was thought that when these markets were no longer available, the Japanese would not be able to continue their expansion into China and Asia more broadly.

Morgenthau was directly involved in trying to fortify China's economy with the intention of helping it to resist Japanese aggression. He convinced Roosevelt to continue the purchase of Chinese silver, thus providing the government of Chiang Kai Shek with the revenue that it required to finance a military resistance to the invading Japanese. In this way, the US dollar was used to prop up the government of Chiang Kai Shek with the objective of mitigating the erosion of United States strategic influence in China.

In addition to this US economic support for China, the United States also contemplated curtailing Japan's expansion beyond a certain point in the Pacific. The Roosevelt administration – and Sumner Welles in particular – planned to "draw a line" in the Pacific, which was to be enforced by the US together with Britain. A large map of the Pacific in the Oval Office was apparently used by the Roosevelt administration to determine where the line should be drawn, however, by October 1937 the exact position of the line had not been determined (Rosenman, 1952).

Although the international tensions that would result in the outbreak of World War II were increasing as the 1930s progressed, in 1936 the United States, Britain and France established a pact. Morgenthau announced the pact on 25 September 1936, which was to strengthen and increase coordination between the major economies that were still on friendly terms. The agreement was a commitment to holding constant consultations over exchange rates between the pound, franc and dollar. The purpose of this approach was to forestall recession in these economies through coordinated action that would allow the respective governments to intervene in the currency markets, thus stopping a run on any of the currencies which would have exacerbated an already fragile situation (Oliver, 1984). Another important factor from the perspective of the United States was that US negotiators would try to maintain the slight competitive export advantage that it enjoyed due to the dollar devaluation of 1934. Gold would also be a critical factor in this agreement.

From the late 19th century until World War II, the US experienced major changes domestically and internationally. The structural changes that would allow the US dollar to be used as an international currency worked in tandem with the internationalisation of the US state. This internationalisation took the form of reproducing capital-friendly policies within the US sphere of influence, which after the 1898 Spanish-American War included Latin America, the Caribbean, the Philippines and Hawaii. As Barry Eichengreen and Marc Flandreau (2012) demonstrated, by the 1920s the US dollar had already become a critical source of liquidity for international capital on a close par with the Pound Sterling. Eichengreen and Flandreau (2012) highlighted the critical importance of the role that the Federal Reserve played in promoting use of the US dollar and more broadly New York as an important global finical centre. What emerges from the literature on this period is that the policies of the US government were undergoing a process of alignment with the interests of large corporations with major private sector interests, particularly the banks. The final step in this process of alignment was the creation of the Federal Reserve Bank, which bound together the financial interests of private banks with the liquidity needs of the US government. As World War II approached, the US was an established international power within the financial and military spheres, despite the effects of the Great Depression. However, as the Welles mission to Europe in 1937 showed, the US lacked clear political hegemony over European powers. The Grand Area policy, which was introduced in 1944 during the Bretton Woods conference, provided the US with a coherent strategy that would revolutionise the role of the US in global affairs.

CHAPTER TWO

The 'Grand Area' and US Dollar Hegemony

This chapter examines events from mid-1939 to the end of the 1945, demonstrating the deliberate planning that went into creating an "American century" (Luce, 1999). This chapter explains how the dollar was established as the world's reserve currency and the enormous power that this conferred on the US. Critical to this pursuit was the Grand Area concept. This plan emerged from a collaboration between the US State Department and the Council on Foreign Relations (CFR) in 1939 (Shoup & Minter, 2004). In establishing US hegemonic influence upon the global economy in the aftermath of the Second World War, the reconstruction programs for Europe and later Japan, in the form of the Lend-Lease program, the Marshall Plan and the Ford Plan, were vital. The most important wartime decisions about the global monetary system were made at the Bretton Woods conference held at the Mount Washington Hotel in Bretton Woods, New Hampshire from 1 July to 22 July 1944. The conference was attended by 730 delegates from 44 allied nations. The economic and financial agreements established at Bretton Woods were the basis of the ability of the US to exercise its hegemony in the post-war period. Critical to US hegemony was the pegging of allied currencies to the US dollar and the linking of the US dollar to gold at a rate of US\$35 an ounce. This later became the basis that permitted the US to draw on the financial surpluses of foreign nations, and it laid the financial foundations for what Charles de Gaulle would call the 'exorbitant privilege' of the United States dollar (Gavin,

2004). This arrangement lasted until President Nixon removed the US dollar from the gold standard in 1971.

The Council on Foreign Relations

The Council on Foreign Relations (CFR), a privately organized grouping of bankers, lawyers and academics, shaped US foreign policy to serve the private interests of US industry (Shoup, 2015, pp. 13-15). The Paris Conference of 1919 provided the impetus for what would become the CFR. Two groups were established that would eventually merge into the CFR in 1921. The first group, established in 1918, was made up of bankers, lawyers and academics, initially comprising 108 members (Shoup, 2015, p. 13). This group met at the New York Club under the name Council on Foreign Relations. It represented the private interests of Wall Street and sought to formulate policies conducive to those interests. This group had become somewhat inactive by 1919, with very few people attending the group's lectures (Grose, 1996, p. 8).

The second group had formed in 1917 when President Wilson organized for certain academics, lawyers and businessmen to study how the US would engage with Europe once Germany had been defeated in World War I in a project referred to as "The Inquiry". Its purpose was to formulate policies for America's post-war relations with Europe. The participants primarily studied the likely effects the peace treaty would have upon American business (Grose, 1996, p. 8). The problems that the 1919 Paris Conference highlighted for American business, combined with President Woodrow Wilson's internationalism, required new ways of thinking and approaching the world. The founding of what is now known as the CFR was the result of a five-month negotiation between these two groups, which began on 3 February 1921 (Grose, 1996, p. 8). In 1921, the intention of the founders of the Council was to prepare the US for the leadership role they believed would be required of the nation in the post-World War I era (Shoup & Minter, 1977, p. 3). Aware that the US lacked the expertise it would need in a range of fields, especially foreign policy, they sought to create a coherent approach that they believed would benefit elite interests within the US. The CFR acted as an intermediary between the private business interests that dominated the group's membership and the US State Department.

The War and Peace Studies Group

A vital planning organization within the CFR was the War and Peace Studies group. Officially named the Studies of American Interests in the War and the Peace, it was integral to the CFR's planning for the post-war peace and it sought to position the US in an advantageous position after the war. On 12 September 1939, leaders of the Council met with Assistant Secretary of State, George Messersmith, to begin post-war planning activities (Shoup, 1975, p. 9):

> In 1939 a group of businessmen, lawyers, journalists and government officials met under the direction of the Council on Foreign Relations (CFR) to find out what the outcome of World War II would likely be and how post war US policy would be carried out after the war.

Messersmith referred the proposal to Secretary of State, Cordell Hull, and Under Secretary of State, Sumner Welles. The plan met with the approval of both Hull and Welles. CFR President Norman H. Davis then gained approval from Hull to begin work on the plan. The Rockefeller Foundation was also involved in the early proposal to offer CFR services to the State Department and contributed $44,500 on December 6 to enable the work to begin. The involvement of the Rockefeller Foundation demonstrated the influence private capitalists would have on the work of the State Department, and the trajectory that planning would take (Domhoff, 2014, pp. 3-4). In mid-December, members of the CFR met at Messersmith's home to determine how this planning would be conducted (Shoup, 1975, p. 10). Study groups were established to specialize in areas that the CFR felt would be paramount to the US during and after the war. There were initially five groupings of analysts, and each studied particular issues that arose during the war and which the analysts felt would be crucial to the post-war period. The five groups were Economic; Financial; Security and Armaments; Territorial; and Future World Organization. However, these were ultimately reduced to four study groups as, shortly after their inception, the Economic and Financial groups were combined (Domhoff, 2014, p. 5).

The War and Peace Studies group was an intellectual – as well as a practical – force behind post-war American hegemony. It envisaged the United States at the centre of the world political system. Despite allusions to "liberal democracy" and "open markets", what was in fact being crafted in the War and Peace group was a strategy that would allow American capital to expand all over the world. Different sections of the world were studied to see how they could best complement – and not compete with – the economic interests of the US. It was seen as particularly important to ensure the reorganization of regional capital in Latin America and other areas of the world to secure US interests (Domhoff, 2014, p. 8).

The Grand Area

Grand Area policy planning was given significant impetus by German victories in Western Europe in mid-1940. Until then, many of the CFR's activities had focused upon organizing the study groups that would conduct planning and other administrative tasks. The German conquest of Western Europe presented new considerations for the planning work of the CFR and the State Department regarding Europe and its German trading partners in Latin America. These considerations revealed the economic objectives that underpinned the CFR's planning work, and indicated a perspective that essentially saw the world as an exploitable resource for American capital accumulation. The Grand Area concept emerged from an awareness of the economic conditions that would be required to support the US economy, as well as analyses of how to deal with the German occupation of Western Europe.

The Grand Area concept was aimed at providing the "minimal territorial living space" necessary for the United States' economy (Shoup, 1975, p. 9). An analysis of the need to build and maintain a Grand Area conducive to US capital required the consideration of economic and military objectives. A vital pillar was the need to foster deeper Anglo-American bilateral relations. The intention was to use the weakened British Empire as a vehicle to promote American hegemony, particularly in the Middle East. Cementing access to Asia was also essential. It was identified that both the US and Britain would need a greater shipping capability to unify and harmonise the Grand Area (Shoup, 1975, p. 22).

The CFR planners realized that control of economically productive areas would be critical to how the Grand Area would operate. Western Europe and Japan were identified by the planners as being central to US economic and geo-strategic objectives. Domhoff (2014, p. 9) explains that the CFR conceptualized the world as comprising four blocs, and sought to analyse the economic strengths of these blocs:

> The council refined its analysis from July through September of 1940 with "detailed study of the location, production, and trade of key commodities and manufactures on a world-wide basis and within the framework of blocs [of nations]". The four blocs were (1) the Western Hemisphere, (2) continental Europe and Mediterranean Basin (excluding the Soviet Union), (3) the Pacific area and Far East; and (4) the British Empire (excluding Canada).

These regional blocs would need to be transformed into complementary markets for US exports. The CFR planners identified these regions as integral to the Grand Area policy due to their strategic importance and their economic suitability as purchasers of US-made goods that could sustain US industry during the post-war years.

The German attack on the USSR in June 1941 added a new aspect to the planning that had been done by the CFR thus far. The biggest change that occurred was in the conception of the Grand Area itself. The planners assumed that a defeat of the Axis powers was only a matter of time. Their defeat would open new opportunities that had not previously been considered. Up until this time, the planning that had taken place considered "the German world" to be essentially off-limits to Grand Area planning. However, with the eventual defeat of both Japan and Germany – two major industrialized and powerful nations that occupied important geo-strategic locations in the world – the planning of the Grand Area could encompass virtually the entire world (Shoup & Minter, 2004, p. 141).

Analysis from the CFR would inform the war aims and strategies of the United States, particularly with respect to the interpretation of the Japanese expansion in Asia. Japan's further penetration deep into South East Asia caused great concern for the Roosevelt administration because of the importance of the raw materials within the region, as well as the fact that it cut off British supplies coming from South East Asia, which affected the British war effort in Europe. In July 1941, President Roosevelt said that, "The US had to get a lot of things—rubber, tin, and so forth and so on, down in the Dutch Indies, the Straits Settlements and Indo-China" (Shoup & Minter, 2004, p. 143).Secretary of State, Cordell Hull, was a major advocate for blocking the Japanese in South Asia. The Under Secretary of State, Sumner Welles, also agreed that Japan's advance represented a threat to the national interests of the US due to the natural resources of the region. At a joint meeting in January 1941, the four study groupings within the CFR's War and Peace Studies group agreed that Japan's incursion into South East Asia would be considered a threat to the national interests of the US (Shoup & Minter, 2004, p. 143). This conclusion reflected the worldview that was emerging within the Roosevelt administration, as well as in the CFR and the US State Department.

Towards the end of 1941, the CFR and the State Department created a special committee to examine the issue of post-war diplomacy. It was named the Advisory Committee on Postwar Foreign Policy (ACPFP) (Rofe, 2012). US Secretary of State, Cordell Hull, gave instructions to Leo Pasvolsky, who was his special assistant, to establish this committee in collaboration with Norman H. Davis, leader of the CFR. Its purpose was to provide the president of the US with policy advice on post-war foreign relations with the rest of the world. It was an extension of the planning work done earlier by the CFR and represented an unprecedented level of integration between the CFR and the State Department. The ACPFP's organization was similar to the study groups established by the CFR in 1939. It was made up of three sub-committees studying post-war topics that were considered important by Hull. They were: armament, political-territorial issues, and trade-financial issues (Shoup & Minter, 2004, p. 148). These issues mirrored closely the priorities that the CFR had identified earlier, but what was different about the ACPFP was its high level of planning within the US government, and its special contact with and access to the president, mostly through Hull.

To integrate the world economy under US leadership, global institutions were needed. The World Bank and the International Monetary Fund (IMF) were created to this end. These institutions emerged out of the policy advice of the War and Peace Studies group at the end of 1941. The US Treasury was also involved in the planning of the two organizations. Although the US Treasury was not an official participant in the CFR planning, there was an obvious need for the input of the US Treasury given the economic and financial nature of the Grand Area. The unofficial liaison between the two departments was Alvin H. Hansen, who worked at the Treasury Department and within the CFR Economic and Financial planning group. The intention of the IMF was to stabilize the currencies and balance of payments of member nations. The legacy of the Great Depression was still strong, and preventing another economic depression was prominent in the minds of the planners. The World Bank would deal with payments not associated with the two main objectives of the IMF. Harry Dexter White of the US Treasury Department undertook detailed planning on these two organizations and submitted the proposal for the creation of the IMF to President Roosevelt in May 1942. Shortly afterwards an interdepartmental committee was established to bring these plans to fruition (Shoup & Minter, 2004, p. 168).

Lend-Lease

In 1941, with the US still officially not involved in World War II militarily, the US provided war materiel and capital loans to Britain. Lend-Lease was the agreement that would facilitate the delivery of these goods and funds from the US to Britain. However, Lend-Lease was more than just an agreement to help an ally in wartime. Examining the inner workings and intentions of the organizers of Lend-Lease, it can be seen that this was a hegemonic project that would implement aspects of the Grand Area for the first time. The Lend-Lease Act, which Roosevelt signed into law in 1941, arose out of the first major agreement between the United States and Britain in the context of World War II. The Act's name stemmed from the fact that goods would be supplied on a deferred payment system: they would be "lent" and then payment would be made at a later date('Lend-Lease and Military Aid to the Allies in the Early Years of World War II', n.d.). It was called "H.R. 1776, An Act to Promote the Defense of the United States", and it empowered the president to provide "defense articles" to allies of the United States. The Act enabled the United States to supply its wartime allies with selected goods on a deferred payment basis.

The Act provided US$2 billion, US$1.3 billion of which was credited to Britain to buy arms from the United States. However, the agreement required that any ships provided to Britain would not be needed for the defense of the United States and demanded written consent from "our highest Army and Navy officers" (H.R.1776, 1941). Britain's need for ships stemmed from the fact that it had suffered heavy losses in the Atlantic from German U-boat attacks. By September 1940, the United States had given fifty obsolete naval destroyers to Britain in return for 99-year leases on British colonies in the Caribbean and on Newfoundland for United States military installations (D.P.E., 1945, p. 55). The legislation compelled Britain to provide other assets in payment for materials provided by the United States, due to Britain's dire economic situation and the inability to pay for goods.

In return for the supply of defense articles, Section 3 of the Lend-Lease Act also empowered the US president to demand a country to pay with rubber, tin, the transfer of defense plants owned in the US or any other direct or indirect benefit to the United States. The compelling need for this provision was that Britain, for example, had only enough assets that could be converted into dollars in both the US and abroad to pay for orders already placed in the US (United States House of Representatives, 1941). Edward Stettinius, who led the administration of Lend-Lease, described the Act as "a new and important development in the foreign policy of the United States" (Stettinius, 1944, p. viii). The development that Stettinius describes can be understood as reflecting a completely new geo-strategic environment that the war had created. In this context, Lend-Lease was the first tangible expression of United States' strategic ambitions over its enemies and allies alike. A critical aspect of the way that the Lend-Lease Act was conceived was that the defense of Britain was considered of "vital importance to the defense of the United States" (D.P.E., 1945, p. 55).

The United States Treasury Secretary, Henry Morgenthau Jr, was critical to the implementation of the Grand Area doctrine. Morgenthau Jr and his department were intimately involved in the strategic planning that had been done before the US entry into the war, and fully supported its objectives. Morgenthau's aim was to shift financial power from New York and London to Washington. The US dollar would become the instrument of a global "New Deal", permitting more socially enlightened economic management. This would require "American financial hegemony", not only to provide adequate export credit, but also to fund the kinds of social welfare planning about which private enterprise had traditionally been unenthusiastic (Hudson, 2003, p. 119). Treasury Secretary Henry Morgenthau Jr, who led negotiations with the British, shared the objectives and worldview that the Roosevelt administration and its planners were pursuing for the post-war world (Skidelsky, 2001). Shoup (1975, pp. 33-34) has explained that theUS aspired to replace the British Empire as the dominant world hegemon in the post war period:

With the entry of the United States into World War II, American planners were virtually unanimous in the belief that the nation should claim a dominant position in the postwar world. As usual, however, the leaders of the Council on Foreign Relations were stating this view most clearly. Council President Norman H. Davis, now Chairman of the Department of State's Security Subcommittee of the Advisory Committee on Postwar Foreign Policy, asserted in early May, 1942 that it was probable "the British Empire as it existed in the past will never reappear and that the United States may have to take its place".

Achieving this objective would require the dismantling of the British Empire, and subordinating it as a "junior partner" of the US. The British Empire was identified by Morgenthau Jr as standing in the way of US hegemony. Morgenthau negotiated with the British with a view to helping the British fight and win, but not to recover their position as world banker or potential rival (Hudson, 2003, p. 119).

Bretton Woods

The Grand Area required that the US abandon its pre-war isolationism. While it is true that the American state had increasingly been internationalizing in the pre-World War II period, the Grand Area concept and its 'living space' requirements added a new strategic dimension to the political reality of the American state and its new role as the core of a US-led world system. The Bretton Woods conference was a pivotal event in the 20th century. From the Bretton Woods conference came the economic structures and agreements that shaped how the world would function until gold–dollar convertibility ended in 1971. Furthermore, the Bretton Woods conference conferred on the US unprecedented hegemonic power. At this conference, the US dollar was instituted as the world's reserve currency. This was done by linking the value of the dollar to gold at $35 an ounce and then setting the convertibility of the currencies of participating nations to the US dollar. The United States, through this arrangement, now had the ability to consume the economic surpluses of foreign nations, thus subsidizing the US economy. This arrangement also allowed the US to export its inflation to foreign nations, which permitted the US to continually inflate the money supply inside and outside the US.

During the 1950s and 1960s, this became a point of contention with the French government, led by President Charles de Gaulle who accused the US of exporting its inflation to his country and others (Gavin, 2004, p. 24). Furthermore, the strength of this system was demonstrated in 1971 when US President Richard Nixon decided to abandon gold–dollar convertibility. This decision could have been seen as a sign of acute and fundamental weaknesses in the United States economy. However, the US was a provider of liquidity to the world, and at the time of the Nixon shock, it was the largest economy in the world, and so it was able to abandon gold–dollar convertibility without incident (Strange, 1987). As the provider of the world's liquidity, the United States could export its inflation, or conversely deflation, by requiring that other nations also revalue their currencies to maintain their value. This is the profound strength of possessing the world's reserve currency. In effect, it became a tool that enabled the United States, firstly, to consume the economic surpluses of foreign nations that were reliant on US capital, and secondly, to export inflation abroad. Domestically, this resolved the problem of how to manage the inflation that had dogged the US in the pre-World War II period.

The International Monetary Fund (IMF) proved to be a vital tool of US hegemony. The US as the largest contributor of funds to the IMF gained the largest share of the votes on the IMF board. This gave the US a de-facto veto over the financial and political policies of member nations. With the ability to block loans, the US was able to regulate the behavior of member nations. This feature was utilized during the Suez Crisis of 1956, a little over ten years after the IMF was established (Hudson, 2003, p. 120). The negotiations over the composition of an international lender that could stabilize currencies also reflected the dominant position of the US. Intense deliberations took place between the US and

Britain about how a fund like this would operate, and its objectives. Harry Dexter White led the negotiations on behalf of the US. White had been a US Treasury official and had a considerable technical knowledge of financial matters. The primary US aim during the negotiations was to open the British Empire to US capital and use Britain, through the city of London, as a way to access the rest of the world (Block, 1977, pp. 59-60).

John Maynard Keynes led the negotiations for Britain. Keynes was in poor health at the negotiations; his case relied on an interventionist model, which gave governments the power to intervene in markets and the financial system. In particular, currency speculation was a key consideration for Keynes, given pre-war currency instability (Steil, 2013, pp. 1-2). The US was able to impose its will on Britain during the negotiations primarily because the US was emerging with an enormous industrial and financial capacity that it had built up during the war (Block, 1977, p. 33). Despite the disparities between the economic position of Britain and the US in this period, a key policy objective for both sides was to maintain full employment. This was a particular concern for the United States, which feared what might happen to US industry if markets could not be found to purchase US-made goods (Block, 1977, p. 33).

To achieve American financial hegemony post-war, US planners would have to reduce the influence of the British Empire. Britain had secured a privileged trading position by establishing preferential trading conditions between Britain and its colonies and the dominions. This imperial preference system also discouraged trade between British colonies and other nations. This was seen as a major impediment to the economic objectives of US strategists. During the Bretton Woods negotiations, the United States attempted to implement the Grand Area policy by pushing Britain to abandon its preferential trading relationship with its colonies.

During the Lend-Lease negotiations between Britain and the United States, the US had formulated two objectives: firstly, the US wanted greater access to Middle East oil, and secondly, it wanted to eliminate Britain as a major international rival to US power. The Bretton Woods negotiations provided the US with an opportunity to achieve these two objectives. The US demanded concessions from Britain, which the British "bitterly" accepted as they had little choice (Callinicos, 2009, p. 169). Nations dependent on US resources for their post-war reconstruction were not in a position to pressure the US politically nor economically. However, the reverse, an extension of US influence over other countries, was clearly possible (Hudson, 2003, p. 138). Economic means would be used to maintain US hegemony over the rest of the world; this was particularly the case in the Western hemisphere. The US wanted to maintain a network of military bases in the region to prevent any nation or coalition of nations from challenging US dominance. US concerns about Soviet intentions were crucial to the decision by the United States to build a military infrastructure in the Western hemisphere (Hudson, 2003, p. 170).

The Marshall Plan

In the aftermath of the Second World War, the United States increasingly assumed a prominent leadership role internationally. The priorities of the US in this period were to counter Soviet influence in Western Europe, and to turn the Grand Area into a consumer market for US goods. Europe was still recovering from the effects of the war and its currencies and gold reserves were insufficient to meet the twin tasks of rebuilding and consuming US exports. The mechanism through which the objectives of the Grand Area would be fulfilled was a plan devised by US Secretary of State George Marshall, known as "the Marshall Plan".

The creation of the Marshall Plan was partly motivated by concerns that war-ravaged Europe could be afflicted by an economic crisis of the magnitude of the 1929 Great Depression. In particular, the US was concerned with preventing the under-consumption of goods, which was one of the factors that had precipitated the Great Depression. Moreover, the Truman administration believed that the lack of US dollars in Europe could lead to another economic crisis in that continent, thus jeopardizing the plans that the US had made before and during the war. By 1947, the year the Marshall Plan came into effect, US hegemony confronted a potential problem. The United States began to fear that European nations, led by Britain, would refuse to use the dollar for continental trade unless a flow of cheap US dollars was maintained. Such a refusal would directly undermine the plans for the Grand Area. The Bretton Woods institutions had not been designed for this purpose and had not been capitalized sufficiently to continually supply a lifeline to Europe, but faced with no other feasible option, the US kept the flow of dollars open to Europe (Newton, 1984, p. 391).

Two of the three leading pre-war industrial nations, Japan and Germany were now under US dominion, the third being the Soviet Union. With Japan and Western Europe now dependent on US capital, a power shift had occurred in these regions in the United States' favor and the US dollar was critical, as Mastanduno (2009, pp. 129-130) explains:

> The U.S. dollar was the lynchpin of the transatlantic and transpacific deal. Freer trade depended on monetary stability, which, in turn, depended on the special role of the dollar. While governments in Western Europe and Japan committed to defending the value of their currencies relative to the dollar, the U.S. government took on the more formidable obligations of maintaining a fixed value for the dollar in terms of gold and of agreeing to accept dollars from other central banks in exchange for gold at that fixed rate. By upholding a pledge that the dollar was "good as gold," U.S. officials provided the confidence that public and private actors needed to embrace the special reserve and liquidity functions of the dollar in the world economy.

The post-'war era had created a new geo-strategic environment for the US, and new opportunities with it. Oil was of critical importance to the exercise of US hegemony. In the pre-war period as late as 1938, much of Europe had still used coal as its main industrial power source (Painter, 1984, p. 361). Two opportunities presented themselves at this point for the US in exerting hegemony over Western Europe. The first was to move Western Europe to an oil-based economy. The second was that as the US was the biggest producer of oil at the time, oil would need to be paid for in US dollars (Groen, 1952, p. 42).

With the objectives of the Grand Area coming to fruition, the moment of US world hegemony had arrived (Wallerstein, 1991, p. 26). Lend-Lease, Bretton Woods and the Marshall Plan represented rapid shifts in global power from Britain to the United States. World War II precipitated this change in global power, providing the conditions which now suited the designers of the Grand Area. Prior to the beginning of the Second World War, the US had already surpassed Britain in terms of economic output, but until it entered the war the US had maintained an isolationist foreign policy. As Wallerstein (1991, p. 26) asserted, World War II marks a divide between the isolationist position of the pre-war US and the post-war Grand Area doctrine:

> At the end of the Second World War, the United States was the strongest economic center of the world economy. It alone had emerged from the war with a very advanced efficient industrial network that had been unscarred by wartime destruction …The moment of US hegemony in the world system has clearly arrived.

The literature that examines World War II, its actors and their thoughts, policies and positions in government, is vast. Laurence Shoup, author of *Imperial Brain Trust*, stated that there is voluminous literature on World War II, but not much attention has been paid to the post-war planning work that was carried out, and the long-term objectives of these planners. While Shoup's work on the diplomatic history of US planners is detailed and meticulous, there is no mention of how the Grand Area would function as a hegemonic construction. There has been an absence of research on the critical role that the dollar played and continues to play in this regard. This chapter has revealed how the dollar has been vital for creating a world system in which the US has been dominant for so long in a situation where it should have experienced a terminal economic crisis. This chapter has argued that: 1) the US had a hegemonic agenda and that it was designed and implemented during World War II, and 2) the dollar has been vital to the exercise of that hegemony ever since.

The planning that began in 1939 marks the start of a coherent strategy that has endured into the twenty-first century. It fundamentally changed how the US and its people saw themselves and their role in the world. This role placed the US at the center of a world system in which it was the most important actor. This change was precipitated by the economic concerns that elite sections of US society held at the time. Their concerns were about currency stability, the Great Depression that was still a recent memory, and domestic factors such as full employment and industrial over-capacity. The world system and the institutions that were created to govern it were designed to meet US domestic objectives. The rest of the world would need to be reorganized economically to suit these objectives, and this reorganization was a prime concern for the planners and underlying this concern were their 'living space' objectives for the US economy. The policies enacted at Bretton Woods were backward looking: they tried to solve the problems of 1920s and 1930s unemployment, currency instability and economic growth to support the US economy and population. By the mid-1950s, new problems had emerged that were unanticipated by wartime planners, and that the Bretton Woods system would be unsuitable for dealing with these problems. These problems included the US deficit needed to finance US troops in Europe, and the paradoxical problem of maintaining the US dollar's world reserve function while it also served its domestic function in the US — the Triffin Dilemma (International Monetary Fund, n.d.).

CHAPTER THREE

Global Fracture

This chapter analyses the period from 1955 to 1974, and considers the 1956 Suez Crisis, the Triffin Dilemma, tensions between the United States and France, and the importance of Saudi Arabian oil to the US. During the Suez Crisis of 1956, the United States demonstrated its growing international economic power. By threatening Britain's deposits at the IMF and the value of the British pound, the United States was able to force Britain out of Egypt, resolving the Suez Crisis and consolidating the United States' growing hegemony.

By the 1950s, the economic consequences of the Bretton Woods agreement had become apparent, and the French were particularly dissatisfied with some of these implications. The convertibility of US dollars held by foreign central banks – especially French banks – into gold became evident as the supply of dollars outside the US began to increase relative to the price of gold. By the 1960s the French government, led by President Charles de Gaulle, felt that France was subsidising the US standard of living and in response France threatened to demand gold for their dollar assets. This chapter also examines another of the unforeseen problems created by the Bretton Woods agreement, which is known as the "Triffin Dilemma".

This chapter explains how the 1974 agreement between the United States and Saudi Arabia ensured that oil trading was conducted exclusively in US dollars from 1974 onward. A brief history of the complex relationship between the US and Saudi

Arabia is provided. The 1974 arrangement between Saudi Arabia and the US was the beginning of the petrodollar phenomenon (Gokay, 2015, p. 10). The fortunes of the US hegemony became inextricably linked with this arrangement, and defending the petro dollar became vital for the US to maintain hegemony.

The 1956 Suez Crisis

By the mid-1950s, the United States could no longer ignore the rise of Arab nationalism in the Middle East, led by Egypt's President Gamal Abdel Nasser. The Eisenhower administration made a strategic decision that Nasser "must be cut down to size" (Venkataramani, 1960). The Middle East region and North Africa were viewed through a global geo-strategic lens, with oil and oil-supply routes considered vital to US interests. Britain was still the dominant hegemon in the Middle East at the time of the Suez Crisis. The Middle East region was increasingly important to US interests in light of the Cold War (Kingseed, 1995, p. 3). Although the US was able to supply its own oil needs domestically, US Secretary of State John Foster Dulles believed that in the event of war with the USSR, oil from the Middle East and West Asia would be essential to the ability of the US to fight and win (Venkataramani, 1960, p. 111). Control of the strategic Suez Canal oil shipping route or "chokepoint" was crucial.

The 1956 Suez Crisis occurred when Egyptian President Nasser nationalized the Suez Canal. This, in turn, prompted an invasion by British, French and Israeli troops. The US objected to this invasion and responded in a unique way that was reflective of the new US hegemony. The US used its financial strength as a means of ending the crisis. The US used the IMF to block British reserves in Egypt, while at the same time the British pound sterling "came under sustained pressure on international markets" that was "viscerally orchestrated" by the US (Andrews, 2006, p. 7). However, until Britain agreed to withdraw its troops from Egypt, the run on the pound that had begun in September of 1956 would continue, leaving the British economy in severe danger.

As the Suez Crisis continued, Britain had a number of concerns in relation to this financial pressure from the United States. Britain feared the inflationary effects of the speculation on the pound, which was being orchestrated by the US Treasury. Britain was also alarmed about the prospect of the cost of oil rising as the value of the pound fell. In 1949, the Bank of England (BoE) had set the exchange rate for the pound at $2.80 (Boughton, 2001). The Bank of England felt that this rate was appropriate to combat the inflationary effects of having to pay excessive prices for oil (Boughton, 2001). However, the US Treasury was able to pressure Britain during the Suez Crisis by selling pounds on the international market. Furthermore, the US refused to lend the British the $1 billion they required to shore up the pound until they agreed to withdraw their troops from Egypt. The US also suspended oil shipments to Britain in order to coerce Britain into a withdrawal (Cooper, 1978, p. 190).

When Britainsought assistance from the IMF to help to break the run on the pound by borrowing capital, these efforts were in vain. The United States was the only member nation of the International Monetary Fund to have a veto over decisions (Hudson, 2003). Britain was unable to mobilize enough votes at the IMF to break the US veto (Boughton, 2001). The United States' veto power was a critical advantage that enabled it to influence IMF decisions. This veto power enabled the US to force Britain to acquiesce to its demands regarding the Suez Crisis. As soon as the British agreed to the terms of the Suez ceasefire, they found that attacks on their currency ceased and the money that they had requested from the IMF was available (Lahav, 2015, p. 1346).

The Suez Crisis demonstrated the strength of the US position in comparison to its allies. The crisis showed that while the US was a relatively new power in the Middle East, it was able to get its way through currency manipulation, coupled with blocking British requests at the IMF. The most important aspect of the crisis from a hegemonic perspective did not take place in the Middle East, even if the invasion sparked the crisis. The currency crisis that the British experienced was orchestrated in New York and

Washington. That the British lacked the capability the sell bonds in order to monetise their way out of their currency predicament demonstrates the supremacy of the US dollar and US financial markets. Although the pound was still influential in world trade, it was used only within the sterling area, making its reach and demand limited. The US, on the other hand, was able to manipulate and issue capital at will by issuing dollars as required and forcing other nations to obtain these dollars through US Treasury bond purchases to maintain parity with the dollar. This would become an issue for European nations in the 1960s.

French Dollar Frustration

The Bretton Woods agreement that established the US dollar as the global reserve currency had some unforeseen economic implications that caused tensions between the United States and France in particular. A contradiction existed between the expenditures of the US government, mostly associated with the defence costs associated with defending Europe and Asia from the USSR, and the convertibility of dollars held by foreign central banks into US gold. As the US dollar was partially pegged to gold at a rate of $35 an ounce in 1944, the US had to run budget surpluses and applied a practical conversion rate in order to maintain confidence in the dollar. A problem with the Bretton Woods system was that it was not anticipated during the negotiations in 1945 that such large defence expenditures would be required far into the future. For example, US defence spending on NATO caused the US to run larger and larger budget deficits into the 1950s and 1960s (Hudson, 2005, p. 22). Such large debts had the effect of reducing the value of US Treasury assets held by foreign central banks. In effect, the US was exporting its inflation to other nations in an attempt to maintain deficit spending. US defense expenditure consumed all of the deficit spending in the 1960s. By 1968, the US gold stock had been reduced to $10 billion dollars, down from $21 billion in 1951 (Hudson, 2005, p. 22).

There was significant contention between the US and France over the deployment of US forces to Europe during the 1960s.

The most pressing issue for the US and Europe was how to pay for the deployment of these forces. The US, France and Britain were concerned about the system of gold–dollar conversion and how NATO and US deployments would be financed. Problems emerged for both the United States and France that spanned the realms of security, finance and defence. French President Charles de Gaulle argued that the international payment system allowed the US to be free from any economic constraints. France threatened to demand gold for its dollar assets. In contrast, US President Kennedy believed that the US financial and military strategy was at the mercy of surplus nations (Gavin, 2002). The problem that both the United States and France confronted was the need to find an effective way to deal with deficits and surpluses in the world financial system.

Countries that produce surpluses require a store of value and security for their surpluses, such as US securities. The US, with its currency pegged to gold, could not run deficits that were too large or disequilibrium would occur between the amount of gold and the number of dollars abroad that could return to the US in exchange for gold. If US deficits had continued to rise there would have been insufficient gold to redeem foreign dollar holdings in the event of a collapse of confidence in the dollar. This problem, known as the "Triffin Dilemma", was highlighted by Belgian-American economist, Robert Triffin.

Triffin observed that the United States, with its domestic currency also serving as the world's reserve currency, would face a balance of payments crisis in the form of gold convertibility (Triffin, 1978, p. 2). Triffin argued that there was an inherent contradiction between a nation using its own currency in world trade and the domestic conditions and policies that it pursued. That contradiction concerns the conflicting demands of exporting inflation abroad through deficit spending and maintaining the value of reserves held by foreign creditors.

US President Nixon dealt with the problem of the gold-pegged dollar by removing the US dollar from the gold standard. The Nixon administration initially did not set out to abolish the gold convertibility system (Trachtenberg, 2011, p. 11). The Nixon administration had expected surplus nations to revalue their currencies upwards. However, the Nixon administration also advised nations that held larger reserves of dollars that requesting gold for dollar holdings would be considered an "unfriendly act" due to the minimal size of US gold reserves (Hudson, 2005, p. 22).

The US Dollar, Saudi Arabia and Oil

The relationship between the United States and the Kingdom of Saudi Arabia in relation to oil is long and complex. Its origins can be traced to the US' recognition of the Kingdom and its rule by King Abdulaziz in 1931 (Blanchard, 2009, p. 3). The bilateral relationship in the pre-World War II era was characterised by a 1933 contract awarded to the California Arabian Standard Oil Company (CASOC), which was formed on behalf of Standard Oil Company of California to develop oil exploration in Saudi Arabia (Kultgen, 2014). This was the first major oil concession provided to the US by Saudi Arabia. By 1938, commercially viable reserves of oil had been found at Dammam Well number seven along the Gulf Coast (Al-Ahmed, Bond & Morillo, 2013, p. 3). In 1944, CASOC was renamed the Saudi American Oil Company (ARAMCO) after the US government nationalised one-third of the company (Mitchell, 2002, p. 17).

Harold Ickes, the US Secretary of the Interior, and Petroleum Coordinator for National Defense at the State Department, advised President Roosevelt that, "It is our strong belief that the development of Saudi Arabian petroleum resources should be viewed in the light of the broad national interest" (as cited in Engdahl, 2004a, p. 88).US energy security, and by extension national security, was now linked with a kingdom on the other side of the world. The United States' mechanised military forces were consuming vast oil resources, and the US had learnt from the defeat of the Axis powers in World War II that this vital commodity would be essential in the operation of the US military. In the immediate post-war period, most of the oil produced in Saudi Arabia continued to be used by the US military. In 1943

Harold Ickes wrote an article entitled, "We're running out of oil", in which he argued, "if there should be a World War Three it would have to be fought with someone else's petroleum, because the United States wouldn't have it … America's crown, symbolising supremacy as the oil empire of the world, is sliding down over one eye" (as cited in Yergin, 2011, p. 395).

The Second World War shifted the global supply of oil to the Persian Gulf region of the Middle East. At the commencement of World War II, "barely 5 percent of the crude oil produced in the world came from the Middle East – 63 percent was extracted in the United States" (Auzanneau, 2018 p. 177). However, after World War II the US "was destined to become a net importer of oil" (Yergin, 2008, p. 377).In 1947, five American oil companies supplied Europe's oil needs. This left Europe at the mercy of US oil producers. US oil majors exploited Marshall Plan funds by charging artificially high prices for oil and shipping it to Europe (Engdahl, 2004a, p. 89). By further limiting the oil capacity of Europe, the US government prevented the use of Marshall Plan funds to expand European oil refining capacity, making Europe dependent on the US oil companies (Engdahl, 2004a, p. 89).

The remittances paid to Middle East governments for their oil were important to the establishment of the US dollar as a critical oil trading currency and ensured US hegemony within the Middle East. In 1949, the Saudi Arabian government wanted to review the concession arrangements with ARAMCO with a view to increasing its share of revenue. To placate the Saudi Arabian government, a deal was done whereby ARAMCO was allowed to offset increased revenues paid to the Saudi Arabian government against its tax liabilities in the US. Odell (1981, p. 36) argues that the US placed considerable importance on the deal:

> The US considered its interests in Middle East oil industry and the way in which it was organized so vital that it was prepared to forgo, on behalf of its taxpayers the large amount of taxes that it had formally been paid by the companies concerned.

This arrangement placated both parties and secured the goodwill of the Saudi government for the continued development of Saudi reserves.

In the 1950s, new threats to US hegemony had emerged in the Middle East and North Africa: Arab nationalism, as well as the nationalist tendencies of the of the Mossadegh government in Iran in relation to oil. The exploitation of oil by Western nations, led by the US in the Middle East and North Africa, generated a significant backlash on the part of populations in the region (Hinnebusch & Ehteshami, 2002, p. 3). At certain times, this backlash manifested in political regimes that challenged Western dominance of oil production. These political regimes took the form of nationalist governments that sought greater independence from Western exploitation. Ba'athism in Iraq and Syria, Khomeini's Iran and Nasser's Egypt all played a role in challenging US domination of the region (Hinnebusch & Ehteshami, 2002, p. 18).

One of the first attempts to nationalise oil occurred in Iran under the leadership of Dr Mohammed Mossadegh in 1951. The threat from a successful nationalisation of oil could have had regional implications for US strategy (Hinnebusch & Ehteshami, 2002, p. 30). Although Britain still controlled Iranian oil at this time, any successful nationalisation of oil by Iran may have inspired similar actions elsewhere in the Middle East. Iran's efforts could have led to a domino effect in the region, whereby the nationalisation of oil could have threatened the ability of US companies to exploit oil reserves in the Middle East (Hinnebusch & Ehteshami, 2002, p. 30). The successful nationalisation of Iranian oil by Mossadegh would have been a blow to the British economy, and the loss of its prestige and power in the Middle East (Heiss, 1994, p. 512). Had Iranian oil nationalisation been successful, Britain would have faced an economic crisis. The resulting loss of dollar revenues would have cost Britain its largest source of US dollar-denominated revenue (totalling $400 million), and risked a British balance of payments crisis (Painter, 1993, p. 2). Britain was in dire economic straits after World War II and had become a debtor nation, which in turn made it particularly vulnerable to US actions in the post-war period (Hudson, 2003, p. 282).

In 1960, the Organisation of Petroleum Exporting Countries (OPEC) was formed. Venezuela and Iran were the primary architects of the organisation (Choucri, 1980, p. 3). There were a number of reasons for the establishment of OPEC, including the persistent fear from oil-producing nations regarding the oil companies' ability to cut prices without consultation. There was also a realisation among more established oil-producing nations that the entry of new producers with lower prices might cut into their established markets. The growing technical competence of the oil-producing nations also gave them the confidence to advance their own interests, despite risking the displeasure of the major oil companies and major oil-importing countries (Choucri, 1980, p. 3). There was increasing friction between oil companies and host nations over remittances paid for oil production. According to Luciani (2016, p. 110), the disproportionate power of the oil-production companies was a source of contention as they held overwhelming control of remittances:

> Oil production in the Gulf before 1972 was controlled by producing companies, or consortia in which the major international oil companies cooperated in a web of interlocking interests... Producing consortia held huge concessions and frequently were the only producers in the country, thus commanding enormous bargaining power vis-à-vis the national government.

Multinational oil corporations played a critical role in extracting oil from Middle East nations and paying royalties to host governments. Their operations also created friction between host governments and US interests. However, a 1975 report to the US Federal Energy Administration (Krueger, 1975, p. 61) suggests that the US adopted a seemingly neutral approach to disputes between oil-producing nations and oil companies:

> Although the multinational petroleum companies were generally able to cope with these problems, their control

over production and pricing decisions was increasingly jeopardized by the nationalistic aspirations of the producer governments and the proliferation of additional firms throughout the international petroleum system. During this period, the US government basically remained in the background and did not attempt to influence or control international supply agreements.

Oil producers were running current account surpluses; this created an increased demand for US dollars as the trading currency of choice, and this favoured the United States. The role of the United States' currency as the global reserve currency provided the US with some unique advantages. Its global reserve currency status gave the US "the capacity to print its currency in exchange for oil and for foreign trade" (Spiro, 1999, p. 4). This phenomenon benefited the US greatly in the oil trade, as Spiro (1999, p. 4) asserts:

> ... this form of leadership also carried with it the potential for exorbitant privileges. If the United States competed for capital unilaterally, and then made other nations come to terms for access to that capital, the result would be predatory leadership that was not in anyone's interest except that of the United States.

By 1971, persistent problems regarding dollar convertibility pushed the United States toward a financial crisis. In 1971, US President Richard Nixon removed the US dollar from the gold standard, stopping the conversion of US dollars into gold. Until this time dollars had been convertible into gold at the rate of $35 an ounce. Levels of US securities that were being held by foreign central banks were becoming unsustainable for the US, which had a currency whose value was fixed to the value of gold. The main reason that Nixon ended the gold standard was that Britain and France planned to exchange their dollar holdings for gold. At Camp David on 15 August 1971, President Nixon instructed the Secretary of the Treasury, John Connolly to stop the convertibility of dollars into gold (Bordo, 1993, p. 80). However, there was a positive for the US dollar: although convertibility had been abandoned, there existed no alternative to the dollar as a viable form of international exchange and reserve medium – the world was now on a de facto dollar standard (Bordo, 1993, p. 74). When Nixon removed the US from the gold standard, a critical structural change in domestic US and world finances occurred. The US dollar was no longer pegged to a fixed physical commodity determining its value, and at this time, the US dollar became known as a fiat currency (D'Arista, 2009).

A secret agreement initiated by the US with Saudi Arabia established an exclusive trading arrangement in 1971 whereby Saudi oil was traded in US dollars. US financial dominance, and by extension political dominance, became contingent on this trade of Saudi oil in US dollars. A unique relationship exists between the trade in oil and the US dollar. The origins of this trade can be traced to bilateral deals between the US and Saudi governments. In 1974 the connection between the trade in oil, which was conducted in US dollars, and US security interests, was formalised "with the establishment of the United States–Saudi Arabian Joint Commission on Economic Cooperation" (Momani, 2008, p. 297). The purpose of this venture was to facilitate closer cooperation between the US and Saudi Arabia with a view to supporting the US economy by promoting the sale of US treasury securities. Critically, the Joint Commission was staffed with officials from the US treasury, which as Momani (2008, p. 297) explains, indicated its importance:

> This Joint Commission also included a special technical group that was staffed by American civil servants who helped US companies to increase their exports to Saudi Arabia. Financed by the Saudi government, the technical group's objectives were to improve bilateral political and commercial relations, promote the export of US goods and services to Saudi Arabia and, most importantly, help recycle Saudi petrodollars through the purchase of US goods.

This relationship was further cemented in meetings between Saudi officials, and US and at this time, it was decided that the Saudi government would invoice all oil sales in dollars, and not a basket of currencies, as had been the convention until then (Momani, 2008, p. 297). The motives of the two sides were very different. The United States General Accounting Office (1984, p. 3) reported that a major benefit to the US would be gained from closer bilateral relations with Saudi Arabia given the 1974 trade deficit that the US was running with the Kingdom. According to Momani (2008, p. 297), the US objective was to get the Saudis to sell oil in dollars only, and then to recycle those dollar surpluses into US treasury bonds, thus supporting the US economy:

> The US–Saudi deal to recycle Saudi wealth into US government bonds was complemented by a subsequent arrangement. Treasury Secretary Michael Blumenthal ... negotiated an enormously successful deal to have the Saudis sell their oil in US dollars. At the time, Saudi Arabia was the key determinant of oil prices, known as the 'oil marker', and its 'Saudi Light Crude' virtually set oil prices for OPEC and non-OPEC oil-producing states. As the largest OPEC producer, the Saudis used their strong influence in OPEC to persuade other members to follow suit; and they did. In 1975, OPEC announced its decision to invoice oil sales in dollars.

This critical deal provided a stable economic foundation for US global hegemony to continue long-term. From 1974 onwards, the ability of the US to run larger and larger budget deficits was facilitated by the fact that the oil trade was conducted exclusively in dollars. While the US had few geopolitical competitors in the 1970s, this deal represented a profound strength. However, as the world became more multipolar, major industrial powers like China and important energy producers like Russia and Iran have integrated into the world capitalist economy. As rivals to the US, these nations recognised the oil trade in US dollars as essentially underpinning US hegemony (Gokay & Whitman, 2004, p. 77).

The 1973 Arab oil embargo was an important milestone in the geopolitics of oil. Some Arab nations threatened to impose an oil embargo against the United States if Israel did not adhere to UN resolution 242, which required Israel to withdraw from territories it had occupied (Tétreault, 2008, p. 8). The use of oil as a political lever had little if any effect on US policy in the Middle East nor upon US support for Israel during the 1973 Arab–Israeli War (Tétreault, 2008, p. 9). The oil embargo was a factor in the cessation of the 1973 Arab–Israeli War (Ilie, 2006, p. 1). The embargo demonstrated a complex set of interdependencies in the relationships between oil producers, OPEC members and non-OPEC members. Arab states had little more than the "oil weapon" to advance their interests. While oil is a critical industrial commodity, the limits of its effectiveness as a weapon were demonstrated by the embargo. Its only power was its ability to constrain supply, thus forcing up the price, and the effectiveness of the embargo lay in the ability of the price rise to inflict severe economic pain on consuming nations, chiefly the United States. US oil companies merely transferred oil from non-Arab producers between themselves so that, while Arab oil did not go to the US, oil from other exporting nations did, thus reducing the effectiveness of the embargo (Ilie, 2006, p. 9). The United States' relationship with Israel complicated its ability to deal credibly with Arab oil producers. Ensuring Israeli security has long been a critical objective for successive US administrations (Khalilzad, Shlapak & Byman, 1997, p. xv).

The 1973 oil embargo came at a time when oil production in the US had reached its peak in 1972 and then begun to decline, making foreign oil supplies to the US more critical than ever, as Parker and Whaples (2013, p. 13) explain:

> Although there proved to be abundant supplies available in the Middle East to replace declining U.S. production, the transition from a world petroleum market centred in the Gulf of Mexico to one centred in the Persian Gulf did not occur smoothly.

The oil embargo was an example of this at times problematic transition. The oil weapon "was a blunt instrument", which "harms friends and foes alike", thus reducing the tactic's effectiveness (Mabro, 2008, p. 2). The oil embargo of 1973 was largely ineffective at securing Arab demands because oil is traded as a commodity that is in global demand and "it is difficult for a seller to isolate a particular importing country and then wield an oil weapon to punish, because oil is widely traded" (Nkomo, 2017, p. 15). Hudson (1996, p. 333) argued that the use of the oil weapon also spurred US initiatives to reduce the tactic's effectiveness should it be used again:

> The shock in the United States and Europe was palpable, and it lent urgency to US secretary of state Henry Kissinger's mediation of the war. In the long term, it also led to a comprehensive new energy policy designed to blunt the oil weapon in the future through the Strategic Petroleum Reserve and conservation measures.

The consequences of the oil embargo were felt within the United States, with long lines at petrol stations a direct result. The US responded by introducing oil saving measures. Several domestic policy changes in the US occurred because of the embargo, such as President Nixon's introduction of a 55 mph speed limit on US highways, as well as other measures designed to reduce oil consumption (Horton, n.d.). Despite these changes, US dollar hegemony was still in place. Dollar hegemony is based on the trading of oil in dollars, and because Arab states did not move oil trade into another currency, petrodollar hegemony was not critically affected.

The period from 1955 to 1974 was a transformative one for US hegemony. This chapter has sought to explain some of the most important international influences during this period, and to describe how the US remained in a dominant international position despite the inherent problems of the Bretton Woods agreement. In the immediate post-World War II period, the international financial structure that supports US hegemony was shown to be fragile. The inherent problems of the Bretton Woods system came into immediate focus. These problems related to US spending on international commitments, particularly NATO (Gavin, 2004). As US deficits kept climbing into the 1960s, the convertibility of dollars into gold became problematic, especially as the Bretton Woods agreement had established the gold price at US$35 an ounce.

As US deficits kept rising the foreign holdings of US treasury securities far outstripped the amount of gold required to support these securities. The US was relying on holders of its securities to subsidise the US economy by continuing to accumulate US treasury bonds and not demand gold in return. When it appeared the French and British might demand gold, the US responded by declaring that, "this would be considered an unfriendly act" (Trachtenberg, 2012, p. 189). The subtext of this stance by the United States was that the US did not have the required gold reserves and was not inclined to revalue gold upwards, which would have reduced the value of US securities relative to gold. The predicament of gold-dollar convertibility demonstrated that the Bretton Woods agreement had not addressed the fundamental problem of managing inflation. Gold-dollar convertibility proved to be unsustainable for the United States given its global hegemonic ambitions in the post-World War II period.

As this chapter has shown, the United States' growing hegemonic influence was evident during the 1956 Suez Crisis. The importance of the Suez Crisis from the perspective of dollar hegemony lay in the United States' ability to pressure its British ally into accepting a political outcome that it did not believe was conducive to its interests (Louis & Roger, 1989, p. 11). The United States' tactic of blocking British attempts at the IMF to seek relief for the pound was a practical demonstration of US financial hegemony made possible by US dominance at the IMF.

The petrodollar phenomenon was a crucial demonstration of US hegemony, based upon the US dollar. The 1974 agreement between the US and Saudi Arabia established the exclusive sale of Saudi oil in US dollars. It meant that nations had to acquire US dollars in order to purchase this oil, and this reinforced US hegemony by creating a demand for US dollars independent of the gold standard. This was a source of considerable economic power for the US. Despite some enormous challenges in the form of large deficits, the United States has proven to be economically versatile, especially by removing the US dollar from the gold standard and forging petrodollar agreement with Saudi Arabia.

CHAPTER FOUR

The Relative Decline of US Hegemony

This chapter examines the key events and issues that had implications for US dollar hegemony during the period from the 1970s until the 2008 Global Financial Crisis (GFC). The purpose of this chapter is to explain how these events and issues had the potential to impact upon the ability of the United States to maintain its global hegemony.

Momentous events in world history occurred during this period. The USSR collapsed, China was integrated into the global capitalist economy and the euro currency came into existence. By the 21st century, the world system had begun to fracture and new spheres of influence had emerged. The immediate post-World War II international landscape had all but disappeared (National Intelligence Council, 2012). A remnant of the Bretton Woods agreement, the US dollar remained the world's reserve currency, even though the global share of trade conducted with the US dollar had declined. While the US dollar continued in its reserve capacity, this chapter demonstrates that the period from the 1970s until 2008 gave rise to some of the biggest challenges that US hegemony has faced.

This chapter explores the debate about whether the Euro could displace the US dollar and its role as the world's reserve currency (Chinn & Frankel, 2007). This chapter also considers the rise of neoliberalism, and key developments related to the Federal

Reserve Board, as well as the emergence of the BRICS nations (Brazil, Russia, India, China and South Africa). Specifically, BRICSdemonstrated not only the increasing multipolarity of the world system, but also the fracturing of the world system. This chapter examines the emergence of this fractured, multipolar world system from 2001 to the 2008 Global Financial Crisis.

Neoliberalism

Neoliberal ideology and its implementation have had a profound effect on the way that the US economy has functioned since it first came to dominate US financial policy. A close relationship was formed between the proponents of neoliberalism and the US government. These proponents included Milton Friedman, Arthur Laffer and Robert Lucas (Harvey, 2005, p. 54). The United States government had funded the right-wing economic research of Chilean economists at the Chicago School since the 1950s to counter leftist politics in Latin America (Fourcade-Gourinchas & Babb, 2002). Its creators saw the ideology itself as the best way of securing individual liberty and economic prosperity for society. The origins of neoliberalism date back to the 1950s and the work of Friedrich von Hayek, but the opportunity for neoliberalism to dominate public policy was born out of the inflation crisis of the 1970s (Centeno & Cohen, 2012). Neoliberal ideology had been confined to the margins of economic thought from the 1950s to the early 1970s, and its rise to dominance required specific economic circumstances as well as the support of particular political regimes.

In the 1970s, inflation became an increasingly large problem for the United States. The inflation of the US dollar was caused by the US-Saudi decision to trade oil exclusively in US dollars. The result was that, on the global market, the price of oil rose 400 per cent. When these enormous capital flows were deposited into American and European banks, inflation became a central issue for economic policy makers (Golan, 1976, p. 216). Keynesian economic theory seemed to have no answers to the inflation and stagflation problems of the 1970s (Hayes, 2008). The post-World War II era, which had benefited Western capital, lasted from approximately 1945 until 1971. By the 1970s, these unique historical circumstances which had led to consistently high growth rates in the Western world had broken down. Harvey (2005, p. 12) argues that by the 1960s, the liberalism of the period immediately after the war, which had given rise to high post-war growth rates, was no longer working. It caused increasing unemployment and stagflation through a fall in consumer demand, combined with an increase in the money supply generated by oil trading carried out exclusively in US dollars.

The Federal Reserve Board

In their different ways, the foreign policies of the Carter and Reagan administrations tried to restore the United States to its immediate post-war power. Since the Carter administration particularly, the United States has been in a reactionary mode aimed at stemming the decline of US hegemony. The loss of the American War in Vietnam, and the wave of uprisings and the spread of "liberation ideology" in the Third World shook the confidence of the United States (Wallerstein, 2006). Many of the key figures in the Reagan administration later held leading positions in the George W. Bush administration. The desire of these figures to restore American primacy drove them to adopt extreme measures. However, the results of their policies only sped up the decline of US hegemony (Wallerstein, 2006).

The world system began to fracture in the 1970s because of Third World nations attempting to achieve a more equitable set of economic circumstances for themselves (Robinson, 1996). As a result, United States foreign policy became increasingly defensive from the 1970s. With the election of Salvador Allende in Chile in 1973, the 1978 Islamic revolution in Iran, and a wave of decolonisation throughout the developing world, the US-centric world financial system was under threat from foreign nations and movements that sought greater independence from the US (McNally, 2011, p. 27). In attempting to respond to these developments, the Carter and Reagan administrations adopted financially punitive approaches. The Federal Reserve Board moved to the forefront of economic planning and the recovery of US economic prospects in the 1980s. During the Reagan administration, the policies of the new Federal Reserve chairman, Paul Volker came to play an important role in the debt crisis in Latin America and Africa (Ocampo, 2014).

The United States' industrial base was in decline, as Germany and Japan emerged as key competitors in this regard by the late 1960s, and competition intensified between these nations during the 1980s. With large amounts of capital moving into the United States banking system, a significant increase in stock market prices occurred. In light of the declining US industrial base, it is possible to see how the US economy shifted from manufacturing and a focus on maintaining full employment to asset price speculation. This was enabled by the US dollar's removal from the gold standard in 1971. With the ability to issue US dollars at a limitless rate, the United States was able to revive its economy, if only on the back of asset price speculation (Mitchell, 2008). This was achieved primarily by raising interest rates to 20 per cent, a move which was intended to reduce the independence of nations seeking economic autonomy. This was known as "the Volcker shock". Raising rates to this level caused vast amounts of international capital to pour into the US, thus propping up the US bond market and dollar. Conversely, it weakened and ultimately broke many Third World independence movements (Engdahl, 2011, p. 288). As this interest rate rise caused capital to rush out of emerging markets and into the US financial system, it boosted demand for US dollars, but it also created economic and financial difficulties across some areas of the globe. The Volker shock ultimately maintained the US dollar and its world reserve function, which was "the key to American financial power" (Engdahl, 2011, p. 287).

When considered in strategic terms, it can be seen that "the Volcker Shock" restored US hegemony and recentralised the world economy around the US dollar and its reserve status. As Hudson (2005) demonstrated, the world was fracturing along political lines, driven by the inequitable economic and financial arrangements of the West, meaning primarily the US. While this may seem to indicate that US hegemony was in decline, Strange (1987) argues that it was actually a demonstration of US strength. The US could abandon the gold standard, yet its currency still retained the global reserve function (Keohane, 2005). This advantage was a structural form of global power, and Strange explains that the US had the ability to control the supply and availability of the world's credit. Furthermore, Strange asserts that the traditional indicators of national wealth such as gold were no longer relevant because the US was the only nation that could issue US dollars, and an overwhelming amount of world trade is conducted in US dollars.

Strange (1987, p. 568) contends that traditional reserves become unimportant when dollars can be produced at will by the United States. Strange (1987, p. 569) describes this as moving from an "exorbitant privilege" to a "super exorbitant privilege". Strange's conclusions concerning the dollar echo those of the former French Finance Minister, Valéry Giscard d'Estaing who argued that the dollar and its reserve status represented an "exorbitant privilege" for the US. Giscard d'Estaing was indignant; he believed that the US economy and standard of living were being subsidised by foreign nations (Eichengreen, 2009, p. 55). Giscard d'Estaing's observation was made in the 1960s, well before the abandonment of the gold standard (Eichengreen, 2011, p. 4). Strange's (1987) characterisation of the US dollar's "super exorbitant privilege" conveys the magnitude of the advantages accorded by the US dollar's reserve currency status: the global economy came to be organised around the US dollar. Although foreign nations may be unhappy with this arrangement, as Giscard d'Estaing's statement attests, there is little they can do short of trying to create an entirely new economic and financial system.

Another important factor arises out of an examination of the dollar's "super exorbitant privilege" status: to maintain the dollar's unique status, the US must keep the world supplied with US dollars. After 1971, the US dollar was produced by fiat. It essentially became a debt instrument used to consume the surpluses of foreign nations. While this was the cause of Giscard d'Estaing's complaint in the 1960s, the post-1971 era of the dollar makes this fiat aspect critical to understanding how US hegemony was maintained in the operations of international financial markets. Although the US Treasury issues bonds, they are sold through primary dealers. The primary dealers are major US banks that sell these government bonds all over the world. In times of crisis, the US dollar is often described as a "safe harbour" for international investors, providing greater strength to the dollar and its reserve currency status (Gourinchas, 2010, p. 6). Private banks offer the US the ability to project its hegemony globally, even when other sectors of the economy are declining.

Alan Greenspan succeeded Paul Volcker as chairman of the Federal Reserve on 11 August 1987. Greenspan's tenure as chairman was marked by financial crashes and economic and financial instability (Engdahl, 2011, p. 304). The deregulation drive started by Volcker was continued and expanded by Greenspan. Hera (2012) argues that Greenspan had a negative effect on confidence in the dollar. Greenspan continually cut interest rates and this facilitated a large expansion of debt and a large increase in the money supply (Hera, 2012). The massive increase in the money supply through low interest rates reduced the value of other countries' dollar-based assets, particularly US treasury bonds, which are the assets most sensitive to movements in US interest rates. In effect, the US was exporting its inflation to the rest of the world, just as Charles de Gaulle had complained decades earlier (Eichengreen, 2011, p. 4).

The Euro

In the 1980s and until the mid-1990s, there existed no significant alternative to the US dollar. Yet, when the euro currency was established in the late 1990s, it was widely speculated that a potential challenger may have emerged to the dollar. Eichengreen (2011, p. 7) argues that there is no reason why multiple reserve currencies could not exist together as they had in the past. However, unlike the US, Europe did not have a centralised political leadership and so it was unlikely that the euro could rival the dollar in any serious capacity, particularly in a time of crisis. Nonetheless, the euro was used by the government of Saddam Hussein to trade in Iraqi oil before the 2003 Iraq invasion, and Clark (2005, p. 29) contends that this was a significant motivating factor for the American-led invasion of Iraq. However, another factor should be considered when examining why the US might allow a potential challenger to the dollar: the co-dependency of the European and American economies.

The extent to which the capital markets of the United States and Europe are interconnected and co-dependent is a factor that potentially explains why the US was seemingly unperturbed by the rise of the euro as a key international currency. Rickards (2011) argues that one of the main reasons that the US allowed the euro to rise in value relative to the US dollar was because the Eurozone represented an especially large market for US manufactured and agricultural goods. Rickards (2011, p. 118) states, "A strong Euro keeps up the European appetite for US machines, aircraft, pharmaceuticals, software, agricultural produce, and a variety of goods and services that the US has to offer". Rickards (2011) explains that the US benefited from a strong euro as, when the euro rose relative to the dollar, the US was able to export more goods and services to the Eurozone because the US dollar was cheaper, enabling European buyers to consume more US goods. Competitive devaluation of the US dollar relative to the euro could be seen as a policy designed to stimulate US exports. Hubner (2007) argues that the US government allowed the rise of the value of the euro relative to the US dollar in order to address the United States' expanding trade deficit. As Hubner (2007, p. 32) concludes, "the rise of the Euro towards the US dollar is the outcome of a deliberate strategy by the United States to deal with its rising trade balance deficit and the explosion of the deficit in its current account". Cohen (2011, p. 48)presents an alternative view, arguing that the US would tolerate the emergence of the EU (and by association the euro), provided that it did not interfere with US designs at a geopolitical level:

But none of this will trigger geopolitical conflict with Washington unless the EU's aspirations begin to spread beyond its immediate neighbourhood to regions more traditionally aligned with the US. The safest bet is that the Europeans will act with restraint to avoid direct confrontation with the US. Arguably, only in the Middle East is there a serious risk of a significant risk of serious tension.

Both Hubner (2007) and Rickards (2011) view currencies as tools of geo-strategic positioning that nations use to compete in order to gain economic and geo-political advantage.

The Collapse of the USSR and the Emergence of Rouble Nationalism

At the beginning of the Cold War, the USSR was seen as a threat by the US and Western Europe. As communism spread, the US grew increasingly concerned at the threat it posed (United States Department of State, 1948). The collapse of the Soviet Union was one of the most pivotal moments of the twentieth century. When the USSR imploded, it was argued by Francis Fukuyama (1989) that the "end of history" had come and that liberal democracy and market economics had won the ideological battle between communism and capitalism. When the USSR ceased to exist, the last impediment to US global hegemony had been eliminated and an era of unipolarity was declared (Krauthammer, 1991). Unipolarity can be defined as the lack of a significant geo-strategic competitor to the US (Krauthammer, 1991). The bipolarity of the Cold War period had ceased to exist, and the United States appeared to be at the zenith of its power, politically, economically, militarily and culturally (Beeson, 2004, p. 1).

The collapse of the USSR had no effect on the underlying dollar-centric structures that gave rise to US hegemony. Moreover, Russia still existed as a separate pole of geo-strategic power. The Russian Federation had come into existence in 1991 after the dissolution of the USSR. While the Cold War that existed from 1917 to 1991 had ended, geo-strategic competition continued between the US and Russia, with the US expanding eastward in violation of an agreement made between Mikhail Gorbachev and Ronald Reagan (Lynch, 2007, p. 61).

The rise of Vladimir Putin to the Russian presidency in 1999 saw the reorientation of Russian policy away from the direction taken during the Yeltsin era. Putin's economic policies put an end to the "shock therapy" enacted earlier in the decade by acting Prime Minister Yegor Gaidar (Desai, 2005, p. 88). While relations did not return to the overt hostility of the Cold War era, Russia was nevertheless viewed by Washington as a strategic rival. This was the period of the Cold Peace between the US and Russia. However, Russia continued its purchases of US treasury securities, which demonstrated the strength and influence of the US dollar.

Russia had come to be one of the most "dollarized countries in the world" (Helleiner, 2008). In the 1980s and 1990s Russians preferred US dollars to their domestic currency due to the economic hardships they endured, first as a result of the collapse of the USSR and then as a result of the "shock therapy" policies of the 1990s. Through the strong global price of oil and gas, by 2004 Russia held $73 billion in foreign reserves, 70 per cent of which were denominated in US dollars (Johnson, 2008, p. 380). By 2008, Russia had accumulated $384 billion of foreign reserves with up to $160 billion denominated in US dollars (Johnson, 2008, p. 380). The Russian central bank had a policy of supporting the US dollar even though there was not a large amount of trade between the US and Russia. The large holdings of US dollars in Russia's reserves were due to the price boom in petro carbons and the fact that the US dollar was the primary currency in this trade. This financial position dates back to the 1990s when the USSR collapsed and Russia underwent market reforms (Johnson, 2008, p. 380).

In 2006, Russia's attitude towards the US dollar began to change. Johnson (2008) argues that there are three currents in Russian politics that have prompted moves away from the US dollar. Firstly, frustrated with US foreign policy, particularly due to the Iraq war, Russia sought ways to become integrated into the US-dominated global economy. Secondly, Vladimir Putin's nationalistic domestic agenda focused on utilising the rouble within Russia and promoted its use internationally. Thirdly, the US dollar's value relative to the euro in 2006 put at risk Russia's financial and economic stability (Johnson, 2008, p. 381). A decline in the value of the US dollar relative to the euro and the rouble meant that Russia's US-dominated treasury assets would begin to lose value. For this reason, in 2006 significant sectors of Russian society, combined with business and government officials, urged moves away from the US dollar. There was a strong desire in Russian political circles to move away from using the US dollar in domestic and international trade. Nonetheless, the US dollar retained its hold over the global economy, despite the inclinations of Russian interests to avoid trading in US dollars.

BRICS

A critical development that has seen the world system move away from that established by the Bretton Woods conference is the emergence of the "BRICS" nations. The group is made up of Brazil, Russia, India and China with the addition of South Africa in 2010. The name "BRIC" was coined by then chairman of Goldman Sachs asset management, Jim O'Neill in 2001. The term was intended to give prominence to these emerging market economies which, it was projected, would have a significant impact on world trade and global growth.

It was their economic growth rates that gave the BRICS nations prominence. By 2000, their combined growth rate exceeded that of the G7 (O'Neill, 2001). These BRICS economies were rapidly industrialising (with the exception of Russia) and exporting large quantities of manufactured goods and raw materials. Russia, like South Africa, is a virtual rentier economy. Russia is almost totally reliant upon its exports of oil and natural gas. Furthermore, the BRICS nations received large amounts of foreign investment from the West. The BRICS nations were able to import substantial Western technology and machinery to achieve within decades a level of industrialised development that had taken the US and Western European nations far longer to attain.

The combined economic output of the BRICS nations had been projected to surpass that of the G6 by 2050, "if everything went right" (Wilson & Purushothaman, 2003, p. 2). O'Neill (2001, p. 1) argued that the G7 framework "should be adjusted to incorporate BRICS representatives". O'Neill's assessment is important in two ways. Firstly, these nations were some of the fastest developing economies of the global south, with purchasing power parity (PPP) for the BRIC nations at the end of 2000 being 23.3 per cent of world GDP (O'Neill, 2001). Secondly, these nations represented the emergence of a multipolar world system that appeared to challenge United States hegemony.

There are significant disparities among the BRICS nations, and their economies and political systems differ greatly. Within the BRICS grouping only China, Russia and India share borders. Relations among the BRICS nations have not always been harmonious and, for example, rivalry and disputes have occurred periodically between China and India (Zhang & Li, 2013). Following the collapse of the USSR, Russia and China experienced increasing border tensions. These tensions were particularly pronounced between 2005 and 2010. China failed to support Russia's actions in the brief Georgian conflict in 2008. Russia has also feared the increasing "Sinofication" of its Far East (de Haas, 2013). Despite the disputes and disparities among the BRICS nations, their rising prominence and rapid economic growth rates had seemingly signalled that the BRICS nations would contest the US-centric world economic system.

China is arguably the most important member of BRICS, and it wasChina's dramatic economic development in particular that lent weight to expectations that the BRICS nations would challenge the global hegemony of the United States. The capitalist transformation of China commenced in the late 1970s under the leadership of Deng Xiaoping (Marti, 2002). The most dynamic development in the world economy over the last 30 years has been China's integration into the global capitalist economy. China's integration began tentatively with a series of meetings between US officials and the Chinese government between

1971 and 1974. Henry Kissinger was sent by President Nixon to engage the Chinese in diplomatic talks on an issue of mutual concern, the USSR. Its brief border conflict with the USSR in 1969 led China to put aside ideological differences and pursue a more pragmatic approach towards the US. In its resumption of diplomatic relations with China, the principal objective of the US was to isolate the USSR by engaging China diplomatically in a so-called "triangular relationship" (Goh, 2005, p. 476). This relationship was characterised, for example, by the US "playing the Soviet card" against China as a diplomatic strategy, before the USSR could play "the China card" in its relationship with the US (Goh, 2005). At this time, Chinese and American relations were characterised by their mutual antagonism towards the USSR. This US-China rapprochement allowed China to become open to Western investment and to begin its steady integration into US world system (Oksenberg & Economy, 1999).

China's economic growth from 1979 to 2018 "meant that on average China has been able to double the size of its economy in real terms every eight years" (United States Congressional Research Service, 2019, p. 5). The expansion of the Chinese economy in this period raised China's prominence in the global economy to extraordinary heights. By the beginning of the 21st century, China had become a major world power. The most important transformation to emerge from China's rapid economic advancement was its geo-strategic competition with the US. One of the most critical developments arising from this competition was the creation of the Shanghai Cooperation Organisation (SCO) in 2001 (de Haas, 2007). The SCO had six founding members, China, Russia, Kazakhstan, Kyrgyzstan, Tajikistan and Uzbekistan. The SCO had evolved from the earlier Shanghai Five grouping and it encompasses most of the Eurasian landmass (de Haas, 2007, p. 7). The SCO represents a loose coalition of interests in Central Asia. However, the Central Asian nations of Kazakhstan, Kyrgyzstan, Tajikistan and Uzbekistan, combined with Russia, possess vast reserves of gas and oil (Javaid & Rashid, 2015).

The increasing influence of China and Russia represent major political challenges to US power in Central Asia, and this has been of particular concern to US planners (Rumer, Sokolsky &Stronski, 2016). The creation of the Shanghai Cooperation Organisation, drawing together different states within such a critical geo-political zone potentially has major implications for how US hegemony in the region will be maintained. Brzezinski's study, *The Grand Chessboard* (1998) provided insight into US motives and views regarding the Eurasian region. Brzezinski (1998, p. 30) stated:

> For America, the chief geopolitical prize is Eurasia. For half a millennium, world affairs were dominated by Eurasian powers and peoples who fought with one another for regional domination and reached out for global power. Now a non-Eurasian power is preeminent in Eurasia—and America's global primacy is directly dependent on how long and how effectively its preponderance on the Eurasian continent is sustained.

Whether the United States can maintain its influence in Eurasia remains to be seen, especially as both China and Russia have sought to establish and expand their own spheres of influence within the region. China and Russia are the major strategic competitors of the US in the Central Asian region (Rumer, Sokolsky & Stronski, 2016). Moreover, China is the region's biggest consumer of oil and Russia is its biggest producer.

China and Russia's views of US influence in Eurasia, and of the role of the US dollar in world trade, are of critical importance. Both China and Russia have already expressed their intentions to move away from the US dollar (Engdahl, 2016). The SCO could provide an alternative multilateral forum for these nations to build cooperation and expand their hegemony in this region. Both China and Russia have sufficiently large economic bases to enable their own currencies to be used for bilateral trade, bypassing the dollar (Aizhu, 2014). China's ascendance as a major economic power has been interpreted by some as representing a profound diminution of US hegemony. Economic cooperation between the influential world powers of China and Russia may have the potential to challenge US dollar hegemony.

CHAPTER FIVE

The US Dollar: the Cleanest Dirty Shirt in the Hamper?

This chapter analyses US dollar hegemony from the Global Financial Crisis of 2008 onwards. No concrete predictions will be offered given the fluid state of world politics and economics. There are an incalculable number of variables at work in the realm of political economy that could affect dollar hegemony and possible alternatives to it. The US government, as well as the geo-political adversaries of the US, have recognised the critical importance that the US dollar has played in the functioning of US foreign policy and the construction of US hegemony.

The importance of the US dollar to the world economic system has led to significant debate about the role the US dollar is likely to play in the future. This debate comprises two broad perspectives. There are those such as Stokes (2014), Fields and Vernengo (2013), Eichengreen (2011) and Prasad (2014) who assert that there will be little if any serious challenge to the US dollar and its reserve status in the near future. They contend that alternative financial institutions have not been developed, and that there is a lack of confidence in the governments of the geo-political adversaries of the US, such as China, Russia and Iran. Eichengreen (2011) argues that because the European Union lacks a unitary political executive, the euro is an unlikely contender for replacing the US dollar as the world's reserve currency.

The opposing argument is that the US dollar is in the process of being replaced in its trading and reserve currency capacities. Proponents of this view, such as Collins (2013) and Roberts (2013a), cite the frustration of geo-political rivals such as China, Russia and Iran. They argue that the nations of China, Russia and Iran feel that using alternatives to the US dollar is one way that they can retaliate against the United States. This potential retaliation tactic is based on the recognition that the US dollar and its status are vital to the continued exercise of US hegemony. The aim of nations such as China, Russia and Iran is to replace the US dollar in bilateral trade, particularly trade in oil, given its critical strategic status. They believe that by replacing the US dollar with their own currencies, or the euro in a basket of currencies, they may be able to extricate themselves from dollar hegemony (Simha, 2016). By reducing demand for US dollars in the vital oil trade, the "petro dollar" and "petro bond" phenomena may be undermined (Simha, 2016). Such an outcome could have catastrophic implications for the US economy and the ability of the US to maintain its ever-increasing budget deficits and national debts.

The notion that the US dollar is approaching the end of its post-Bretton Woods status and special oil trading status has been advanced by Roberts (2013a), Doran (2012) and Clark (2005). These authors base their assessments of the US dollar upon the geo-strategies of rival nations that seek to undermine the influence of the United States and promote their own currencies in important regions of the world. China is one nation that has adopted such strategies in regions including the Middle East, and Central and South Asia. In its trading relationship with Russia, China has aimed to operate both unilaterally and bilaterally. Examples of this strategy include Russia becoming China's largest source of crude oil, and Russia's willingness to accept payments in yuan (Panko, 2016).

Proponents of the argument that the reign of the US dollar will end emphasise the emerging spheres of influence within the world and claim that this will negate the need for a global reserve currency. These spheres of influence could potentially solve problems for competitor nations that possess neither sufficiently developed currency markets nor the institutional and political capacities needed to promote their currencies to the same levels of global usage as the United States. Bilateral trade or trade within these smaller spheres of influence would not require the type of deep liquidity in currency markets and payment transfer systems that are necessities for trade in global markets. Smaller-scale arrangements such as these have typically been made with the intention of pushing back against the geo-political dominance of the US (Koenig, 2016).

The Global Financial Crisis that occurred in 2008 brought into sharp focus the state of the US economy and its finances. The GFC demonstrated the importance of the US financial system in relation to the rest of the world. The GFC also demonstrated the resilience of the US dollar as a major reserve currency. US hegemony had been in decline for decades (Hudson, 2005). The GFC demonstrated the strong financial appeal of the US for international investors. The US dollar's function as a form of "safe harbour" during the crisis was apparent as international investors flooded the US with capital, fearing instability in foreign markets (Noeth & Sengupta, 2012, p. 461). This influx in foreign capital caused the US dollar to increase in value while other currencies such as the Brazilian real and the South African rand depreciated significantly (Nissanke, 2009, p. 11). Nonetheless, during the GFC the movement towards multi-polarity in the world system continued.

In exploring the debates about the future of the US dollar, an important aspect that has been highlighted concerns institutional arrangements. Existing multilateral institutions that are outside of the political control of the United States have been strengthened. New multilateral institutions have been created, such as the Chinese-led Asian Infrastructure Investment Bank (AIIB), and the United States is not included among the AIIB member nations.

The Russian-led Collective Security Treaty Organisation (CSTO) is a multilateral military organisation and has been characterised as a Russian-led NATO (de Haas, 2015). The CSTO and the Shanghai Cooperation Organisation (SCO) are military security organisations that are dedicated to counter terrorism and the collective security of their members. Both are multilateral organisations, outside the influence of the US, that have drawn their membership from nations with critical energy resources. Zbigniew Brzezinski (1998) emphasised the importance of Eurasia to US primacy, and argued that attempts should be made to maintain US hegemony in Eurasia for as long as possible. Brzezinski (1998, p. xiv) stated that it is imperative for US power in Central Asia "that no Eurasian challenger emerges, capable of dominating Eurasia and thus also of challenging America". However, by establishing these multilateral organizations, China and Russia have demonstrated that they may indeed be capable of challenging the international influence of the United States. Moreover, in 2014 it was proposed that the SCO and the CSTO should combine, which could have represented a potential consolidation of power and influence.

Arguments against US Dollar Collapse

Predictions of United States dollar collapse have been made before. In 1968, Ernest Mandel had predicted a dollar crisis for the United States. Mandel was partially correct; there was a crisis in 1971 when Richard Nixon removed the United States dollar from the gold standard as there were existing problems with gold to dollar convertibility. A lack of physical gold meant that the United States could not possibly redeem dollars for gold. Rickards (2011, p. 85) argued that,

> If the price of gold was too low, the problem was not a shortage of gold but an excess of paper money in relation to gold. The excess money was reflected in rising inflation in the United States, the United Kingdom and France.

Stokes (2014) contends that fears of a loss of US hegemony, and perceptions that the US was on the verge of a dollar collapse, are overblown. He asserts that, despite the economic problems of the US such as persistently high national debts and deficits, US allies have little incentive to abandon the dollar. Furthermore, he argues that geopolitical adversaries of the US also have little reason to discard the dollar. He believes that US allies such as Japan and South Korea have no incentive to fundamentally challenge the current financial architecture given their security reliance on the US, and that challengers to US primacy in Asia also have little incentive to disrupt the status quo given the complex and integrated nature of financial economic relationships (Stokes, 2014). Similarly, Kirshner (2008) argues that the likelihood of a US dollar collapse is overstated. He argues that predictions of dollar decline have been made before and have proven incorrect. Like Stokes, Kirshner (2008) points to the lack of alternatives to the dollar as the main reason that the dollar continues in its reserve capacity.

Eichengreen (2011) is an analyst who believes that there is little possibility of the US dollar losing its reserve status. He asserts that, while the United States has experienced economic distress, its enduring strength lies in the belief that the US has fewer problems than any potential rivals. While the US may experience domestic problems, they pale in comparison to the internal problems of its potential rivals. The US still possesses the largest economy and the largest and most liquid financial markets, and it has favourable population demographics, with rising birth rates (Eichengreen, 2011, p. 8). Eichengreen's analysis relies upon the notion that there is no good alternative to the US dollar. Eichengreen (2011, p. 7) notes of the euro that,

> The euro is a currency without a state. When the euro area experiences economic and financial problems, as in 2010 there is no powerful executive branch with the power to solve them.

As Eichengreen observes, this could be present a major obstacle to the euro ever becoming an effective currency alternative to the US dollar. When economic crises arise, for example, decisive political responses are required, not protracted negotiations. Policies and decisions regarding the euro would likely require the achievement of consensus amongst disparate European nations. In contrast, when China or the United States needs to make a decision or implement changes, the approval of the states in the US or the provinces in China is not required before these states can take action. China and the United States, therefore, are much more capable of rapid reactions to economic crises. This capability, too, could have a positive effect upon investor confidence.

Eichengreen (2011) raises the possibility that multiple reserve currencies could exist simultaneously. For several reserve currencies to exist as international mediums of exchange without discord, there would need to be a world system within which no country could use its currency to further its own strategic interest. Like Eichengreen (2011), Fields and Vernengo (2013) argue that neither the Chinese yuan nor the euro meet the requirements to be granted the status of acting as the world's reserve currency. Fields and Vernengo (2013) focus primarily on the euro, as they believe that the euro is unable to perform the same risk-free asset role that they claim the US dollar performs.

Fields and Vernengo's (2013) interpretation of the euro is informed by their belief that the European Union is unable to exert the political and economic influence required to challenge the United States within the structures of the US-dominated world economy. The US had seized the opportunity to establish dollar hegemony through the institutions and arrangements of Bretton Woods in the aftermath of the Second World War. However, no crisis of an equivalent magnitude has arisen to dramatically alter these arrangements, or to cause the euro to be adopted as the global reserve currency. While the European Union does possess deep and liquid financial markets and well developed financial institutions, it has been unable to achieve a broader international currency hegemony with the euro.

Since the 1970s, China has been on a rapid trajectory of economic development, and has become integrated within the global economy. There has been debate and speculation in recent years about the possible role that the Chinese yuan might play as a reserve currency in place of the US dollar. Critics that cast doubt on the potential adoption of the yuan as a reserve currency cite the fact that the yuan is not a free-floating currency. This makes the yuan unsuitable to hold the same status as the US dollar, given that it is difficult to acquire. Furthermore, Chinese financial institutions lack the scale of their US counterparts. This situation has its roots in the export-led development that China has pursued since intensifying its trade with Western nations in the 1970s and particularly the 1980s. To function as a reserve currency in place of the US dollar, the yuan would have to be floated on the open FOREX market, making it freely convertible by nations and companies wishing to use it. However, floating the yuan in this way is only one concern identified by those who doubt the ability of the yuan to supplant the dollar.

China is the largest non-US holder of US Treasury securities, and this has been identified by some analysts as a reason why the Chinese government would not want to see the yuan appreciate in value. Some hypothesize that if the yuan were to be transformed to a free floating currency, the value of US Treasury securities would depreciate and thus the Chinese would lose large amounts of value that they had invested in these assets. However, there is a critical problem with this scenario. Murphy and Yuan (2009) argue that China is a long way from making the yuan an international reserve currency that can rival the US dollar at any point in the near future. It is believed that if the value of the US dollar fell, China would lose a large amount of wealth due to its US Treasury holdings. Murphy and Yuan (2009) assert that:

> ... Beijing has accumulated around 1.4 trillion in U.S. dollar reserves and is keen to avoid any precipitous decline in the dollar's value—which would in turn devalue its own holdings.

While it would seem likely that China would lose a large amount of the value of its US assets by the full liberalisation of the yuan, it has been noted that the Chinese have been steadily increasing their purchase of gold in recent years (Hewitt, 2014). For the People's Bank of China, gold acts as a means of storing national wealth. Moreover, the price of gold would likely increase as well if a fall in the demand for US dollars was to occur. If there was a decline in demand for US dollars, the reaction from investors and international capital markets could result in the diminution of US dollar hegemony. Without the stability provided by the US dollar as the global reserve currency, capital markets worldwide could experience an uncontrollable financial crisis.

Arguments for US Dollar Replacement

There are several aspects to the argument for the short- to medium-term replacement of the US dollar as the world's reserve currency. If the dollar were to be replaced it is expected that the US would lose a fundamental lever for maintaining its dominant position in the global economy. Advocates for this argument generally share the following beliefs: firstly, that foreign holders of US Treasury securities want to replace the US dollar as a bilateral trading currency for a variety of reasons, primarily economic and strategic; secondly, that substituting the dollar as the world's reserve currency is one way that nations can resist United States hegemony; and finally, that nations want to trade in oil without using the US dollar.

A key advocate in this regard is Paul Craig Roberts, who was the Assistant Secretary of the Treasury for Economic Policy during the Reagan Administration from 1981 to 1982. Roberts has written extensively about the US dollar, and as a former high-level employee of the Treasury he has a very good understanding of the functioning of the dollar as the world's reserve currency. Roberts asserts that United States hegemony is fundamentally reliant on the dollar remaining the world's reserve currency. He highlights the ability that the dollar's reserve status grants the US. He argues that protecting its status is vital to the US's continued ability to wage wars, and to run large budgets and national debts without economic problems.

Roberts asserts that protecting the reserve status of the dollar is critical for the US. Roberts (2013b) links the dollar to the ability of the US to be a superpower. In this scenario, keeping the dollar as the world's reserve currency is essential for the continuous exercise of United States power in the world. This view is based on the notion that forcing foreign nations to trade in the dollar will keep US bond yields low and thus not place an unsustainable burden on US financing. However, Roberts believes the continued use of the dollar as a reserve currency will not halt its decline. He argues that large Asian trading partners of the US cannot continue to accept depreciating dollars in exchange for goods and services that they supply to the US. Roberts contends that China is seeking to foster its own domestic market as a means of boosting economic growth and lessening its dependence on being an export nation. Roberts (2007) asserts, too, that Japan hopes that it will be able to more deeply participate in East Asia's economic development if the US dollar's dominance is ended.

The possible decline of the US dollar in oil trading is one of the most contested aspects of the debate concerning the weakening of the dollar. Energy has proven to be a crucial sphere for the operations of US dollar hegemony. However, it has been argued that if geo-strategic competitors can substantially replace the US dollar in this vital trade, then the ability of the US to remain the dominant hegemon will be critically undermined because the demand for US dollars will decrease, causing US interest rates to rise and making debt servicing more expensive for the US. China, as a large consumer of oil and a geo-strategic competitor of the US, is often considered the most likely challenger to the US in this regard. Oil trading in the yuan is seen to be of critical importance in this debate. There are two important considerations with respect to the potential for yuan-denominated oil trading. The first is that by trading oil in the yuan, China will be able to internationalise its currency on a bilateral basis with important oil trading nations such as Russia or Saudi Arabia. Secondly, oil trading in yuan would undermine the petro dollar by threatening the Saudi–US deal of 1974.

Collins (2013) argues that the gradual replacement of the US dollar in oil trading has the capacity to critically undermine the economic position of the United States. China's rapid economic development since the 1990s has been conducted through the use of the US dollar. Recently, however, China has gradually been replacing the US dollar in their bilateral oil trade with Russia. In the post-GFC period, when the United States has continued to experience economic problems, this development has the capacity to deal a powerful blow to United States' economic position in the coming years. Collins emphasises the deteriorating industrial base of the US and the collapse of its housing market as critical economic weaknesses (Collins, 2013). With the US economy and financial system being supported by the Federal Reserve, challenges to the dollar's reserve status would be unwelcome developments. Collins explains that the US now faces a fundamental problem: it consumes more than it produces and exports. In the immediate post-World War II period the US had been a major exporter and the US dollar was a feature of the post-war financial system. However, with the US in an export deficit in the aftermath of the GFC, the trading partners of the US have had to accept depreciating dollars for their exports (Collins, 2013).

Fields and Vernengo (2013) point out that for a currency to achieve reserve status it must be used in oil transactions. The then Iraqi President Saddam Hussein had attempted to replace oil trading in dollars with euros. Clark (2005) argues that this approach is one way that nations could defy the dictates of Washington:

> It is now obvious the invasion of Iraq had less to do with any threat from Saddam's long-gone WMD program and certainly less to do with fighting international terrorism than it has to do with gaining control over Iraq's hydrocarbon reserves and in doing so maintaining the U.S. dollar as the monopoly currency for the critical international oil market.

The underlying US motive was to shore up the dollar and its reserve status. Clark (2005) reveals that maintaining the US dollar and its petro currency status is a geo-strategic imperative, even amongst enemy nations. Iraq stood to earn a large economic surplus if it moved its oil payments to euros. Engdahl (2004b) argues that preventing this occurrence was one of the main factors motivating the Iraq war of 2003. He emphasises that American hegemony depends on the petro currency phenomenon established in the 1970s. Engdahl (2004b) explains that the Iraq war was one way of warning other nations not to abandon this system:

> All indications are that the Iraq war was seized on as the easiest way to deliver a deadly pre-emptive warning to OPEC and others, not to flirt with abandoning the Petro-dollar system in favour of one based on the euro.

Like Engdahl, Clark (2005) argues that the United States' decision to invade Iraq was largely motivated by the desire to maintain the US dollar as the primary currency for the trading of oil. Clark (2005) analyses the US dollar in the context of United States' foreign policy. In Clark's (2005, p. 21) view, the policy actions of successive US governments beginning with the 1973 oil shock have been motivated by the necessity to maintain the US dollar as the primary trading currency for oil. It is important to take into consideration that it costs the United States very little to issue US dollars and Treasury bonds, however,a foreign nation must produce real value relative to the US dollars it wishes to acquire. This is how the United States' economy is subsidised by much of the rest of the world, and why any shift away from the US dollar would represent a tangible threat to the United States' economy and its hegemonic power in the world.

The debate regarding the potential replacement of the US dollar reveals that the dollar's status is vital to US dominance. US dollar hegemony requires the participation of other nations in the US dollar-centric structures of the world economy, and large trading countries such as China and Russia with major capital requirements are particularly important in this regard. China, for example, has accumulated substantial US denominated securities. A question often overlooked by analysts who contend that the US dollar's future is assured is how much longer China will hold US securities, particularly in a low interest rate environment and with inflation outstripping US bond yields. Holders of US dollar-denominated securities are losing capital to the US through low interest rates, and this arrangement is not sustainable in the long term.

Prasad (2014) and Stokes (2014) argue that the US dollar is secure for now, given the lack of an alternative for the role of the world's reserve currency. However, their arguments are based upon the perpetuation of an interconnected world system with a dominant hegemon using its currency and institutions to regulate world trade. As a more multipolar world system has emerged, the currencies of other nations are becoming more prominent in global trade. The *Global Trends 2025* report states that the "international system—as constructed following the Second World War—will be almost unrecognizable by 2025" (National Intelligence Council, 2008, p. 1). Moreover, spheres of influence centred on large market-oriented states are having a major impact on how the global economy operates and how power is distributed and projected.

Another aspect of the debate about the demise of US dollar hegemony concerns the international payments system through which global trade is conducted. Currently, the world's banks trade primarily through the Society for Worldwide Interbank Financial Telecommunication (SWIFT) system. This confers a large amount of power on the nations that control this institution, primarily the US. Iran, for example, was one nation that was excluded from the system due to international sanctions, thus isolating Iran completely and preventing it from accepting payment for its foreign trade (Arnold, 2016). China has shown interest in establishing an alternative to the SWIFT system, and has been developing the China International Payment System (CIPS). This system will be outside the control of the US and is an avenue for nations to settle bilateral payments. CIPS would help to continue the internationalisation of the Chinese yuan as an important trading currency (Waldau, 2015). This system could streamline what has been a difficult method for using the yuan to settle payments. The development of CIPS could undermine a key aspect of US financial hegemony. By establishing a competing system, China could create the infrastructure necessary to challenge the dominance of the US dollar.

In the 21st century, the geo-strategic competitors of the US are establishing multilateral financial and economic projects that are independent of the US. These institutional developments represent tangible ways in which US hegemony is being challenged. The development of China's New Silk and Maritime Roads, which together are termed the "One Belt One Road" (OBOR) project, in conjunction with the Asian Infrastructure Investment Bank (AIIB) and SCO, along with Russia's CSTO, represent a continued fracturing of US global hegemony. The internationalisation of the yuan as a global reserve and trade currency through bilateral currency swaps and transmission through the AIIB represent powerful trends that present alternatives and challenges to US hegemony.

China's OBOR project is vast in its conception, and will integrate Eurasia and other crucial regions into China's economic and strategic orbit. The OBOR project aims to build 3000 km of road, rail and pipelines over the next 15 years (Zimmerman, 2015). The OBOR involves several intersecting strategic objectives for China. The first is to diversify energy supply and energy transport to China away from the US-controlled Strait of Malacca. The second objective is to make nations such as Iran, Pakistan and Afghanistan politically important to China, given the importance that the United States places on these nations for its own geo-strategy. These three nations were recently granted observer status at the SCO and may become members in future (Putz, 2016). The third objective is to give China greater and more secure access to the Middle East. The OBOR initiative would also give China a larger market for its goods and services.

Thousands of kilometres of rail line built by China will integrate the Eurasian region. On 23 January 2016, Iran's President Hassan Rouhani and China's President Xi Jinping signed a $600 billion railway plan to link Iran, Shanghai in China and Western Europe (Sputnik, 2016). The deal represents a significant development in relations for both nations. The deal is an important one for Iran at a time when US-led efforts have isolated Iran politically and economically. From China's perspective, the Iran deal represents a potential blow to US efforts to quarantine Iran.

China's OBOR initiative also extends to the vital energy sphere. As part of the OBOR project, China has plans to construct a pipeline that will run from Iran through Pakistan and into Western China. This project has been opposed from the beginning by the US because it is counter to its strategic interests (Cohen, Curtis & Graham, 2008). Energy security and domestic economic concerns are the driving force in China's approach to Central Asia. In the 1980s China was self-sufficient in oil, however, given its rapid industrialisation and economic development in recent decades, China has become dependent on energy imports. In an attempt to mitigate its reliance on oil from unstable regions like the Middle East and Sub-Saharan Africa, China is attempting to diversify its supplies.

China aims to become less reliant on Russian energy supplies in spite of large deals that have recently been signed (Brugier, 2014, p. 4). China is reluctant to further deepen energy ties to Russia because China is prevented by Russian policy from making investments or taking on partnership agreements with Russia in respect to energy development (Brugier, 2014, p. 3). China would prefer to bypass Russia by directing its trade with Europe along the OBOR corridor through Central Asia. Russia sees itself as the dominant power in Central Asia, and China has been cautious about not granting Russia too much leverage by allowing its trade routes to go through Russia (Brugier, 2014, p. 3). There is an obvious strategic concern on the part of the Chinese over granting Russia the ability to potentially disrupt the flow of Chinese trade (Brugier, 2014, p. 3). By building, this vast OBOR project, China hopes to create an integrated sphere of influence based on economic cooperation. With the OBOR project shifting the strategic focus from water to land and creating a vast inland corridor, China is creating a strategic zone that challenges the dominance of the United States (Brugier, 2014, p. 4).

Within the debates about the future of the US dollar, there is much speculation about China's currency, the renminbi (RMB).

An important recent trend that is still emerging has been the internationalisation of the renminbi as a trading currency. As the RMB grows in international prominence, there is speculation about how this could affect the role and primacy of the US dollar in international trade. Despite the size of the Chinese economy, the RMB has made up only a fraction of international trade. As a trading currency, the RMB can be used to make bilateral trade payments. China has been engaging in a multitude of currency swap agreements globally. Since 2009, China has signed currency swap agreements with 32 countries. This helps to advance the RMB as an international currency and also promotes Chinese penetration into important regions of the world such as the immediate Asian region and the Middle East (Steil& Walker, 2015). Greater internationalisation of the RMB would increase competition with the US dollar. China's approach in this regard is to work cooperatively within the US-led world economic system while simultaneously creating parallel structures and institutions, such as the Asian Infrastructure Investment Bank (AIIB). Such institutions are designed to increase Chinese autonomy and freedom of action in comparison to the existing institutions dominated by Western nations (Heilmann, Rudolf, Huotari&Buckow, 2014).

The debates regarding the US dollar's future as the world's reserve currency will continue. The largest foreign holder of US securities, China, has reportedly stopped purchasing US Treasury bonds in an effort to boost its own currency (Gillespie, 2016). There is also concern in Russia over the role that the US dollar plays in US hegemony, and Russia has taken steps to replace the US dollar in its oil trade with the rest of the world (Engdahl, 2016). China's OBOR project is likely to vastly increase China's influence in different regions of the world. The continued internationalisation of China's RMB, too, potentially poses a tangible challenge to the US dollar. However, among the existing world currencies that have the potential to act as the global reserve currency, it appears that the US dollar is the equivalent of the "cleanest dirty shirt in the hamper" (Schiff, 2015).

Conclusion

The central argument of this book is that the United States dollar has been vital to the exercise of hegemony in the post-World War II era. There are two main reasons for making this claim. The first is the political motive with evidence that planners inside the US government, and closely associated with the Council on Foreign Relations (CFR), made plans to pursue a hegemonic agenda in the post-World War II era, the Grand Area. The evidence, in the form of original source documents compiled by Laurence Shoup and William Minter (2004), demonstrate this well. The second reason for making this claim is the financial aspect. This section of the argument is reliant on a reconceptualization of the dollar as an instrument that allows the US to function in a hegemonic way. Of particular importance in making this argument, and offering it as a legitimate explanation for dollar hegemony, are two key moments in history. They are the Bretton Woods conference of 1944 and the US-Saudi relationship agreed to in 1974. Both these moments in post-war history are instructive in presenting a convincing case for dollar hegemony. First, the Bretton Woods conference positioned the US at the centre of the world in economic terms and established the World Bank and International Monetary Fund, the most important structures in world finance (Engdahl, 2011). Second, the 1974 agreement between the US and Saudi Arabia created the petro dollar and petro bond. Forcing nations to acquire dollars to purchase oil created a massive demand for US dollars. This agreement, which still exists, demonstrates the economic power of the United States. It also demonstrates that the world is still contingent on US actions in the world economy. This agreement shows the extent to which Saudi Arabia was integrated within US financial and security systems. By linking the US dollar to Saudi Arabian oil, extremely close ties were forged between these two nations.

The second major theme that emerges from the research is the balance of payments question. Crises regarding the balance of payments have been recurring. The dollar went from strength to strength, recovering from each successive crisis, beginning with the 1907 New York share crash and continuing to the 2008 financial crisis. Even prior to the 1907 crisis, the 1893 gold hoarding crisis began to draw private banks and the US government closer together, eventually leading to the creation of the Federal Reserve in 1913 (Engdahl, 2011, p. 34). Ongoing crises have allowed the dollar to strengthen its position each time. This is due to two factors. The US possesses a large and liquid financial system in the form of private banks, supported by the Federal Reserve. This ensures they can rapidly deploy capital, if only between themselves and European and Japanese banks. The second factor in there is no alternative at this stage to the dollar. There are debates over the merits of gold reserves and special drawing rights (SDRs). However, in times of crisis, private banks and investors demand immediate action on the part of government, as evidenced in 2008. The 2008 crisis represented a banking crisis, with overleveraged banks indebting themselves beyond the value of their assets. With such large government bailouts of the banks, it may yet produce a sovereign wealth crisis, with government debt becoming the cause of crisis. The effect of this scale of crisis could potentially lead to a trade war or a possible new Bretton Woods conference, and nations with large stockpiles of gold would have a significant advantage in any negotiations.

The United States was already a major economic power prior to World War II, but the aftermath of that war saw the US become one of the world's major creditors. The balance of payments between Europe and the US was a significant issue both before and after World War II. During World War I, Western governments amassed large debts to finance their war spending (Higgs, 2005). Soon after the Bretton Woods conference in 1944, the balance of payments with Europe again became a problem. Gavin (2004) demonstrated how the cost of US deployments to Europe during the Cold War increased the balance of payments with Britain and France in particular.

The balance of payments crisis led the US to abandon the gold standard in 1971. Since this time, the world economy has operated on a US dollar standard with an ever-ballooning US deficit. Despite this, some argue that the ability of the US to abandon the gold standard in fact reflected US strength (Strange, 1987; Keohane, 2005). Even after the 2008 crisis, the US dollar strengthened its role as the world's reserve currency, just as it had after the 1971 crisis. The status of the US dollar is not unassailable. However, so far the US dollar has demonstrated its endurance in the world economy, as well as its resilience to crises of differing kinds and the lack of a viable replacement, or unwillingness of foreign governments or corporations to find a substitute. The US dollar's entrenched position may, therefore, be its ultimate advantage.

It is important to consider the geopolitical situation regarding the dollar. Since the 1970s, the US has experienced a decline in its absolute hegemony; this is most noticeable when compared to the period from 1945 to 1970 (Hudson, 2005). This is due to several major changes to geopolitics. These changes include the independence of former European colonies, the integration of China into the world economy and the increasing technological parity of competitor nations to the US, such as China and Russia. After the Soviet Union collapsed in 1991, US world hegemony seemed secure (Krauthammer, 2002). However, as the world has become increasingly multipolar, the US has experienced a relative or marginal decline in its hegemony. In the contemporary context of multipolarity, the US has had to consider a variety of views and actors in the world system. Examples of this include the lack of support for the US war against Iraq in 2003, which forced the US to withdraw a resolution for the war in the UN Security Council (Chomsky, 2003). Another example is efforts by the US to prevent other nations from joining China's Asian Infrastructure Investment Bank (AIIB) (Wihtol, 2015). Nevertheless, the

US dollar continues to be the world's reserve currency as well as the primary oil trading currency. This indicates that if US hegemony is to be seriously challenged a fundamental change in the organisation of the world economy and its associated financial structures has to occur.

The central question concerning the US dollar remains unresolved: how long can the US dollar remain as the world's reserve currency? How much longer this system can continue is unknown and predictions to gauge this possibility have proven wrong in the past. The US dollar has held a unique position in world economics since World War II, and it remains the most important currency through which global trade is conducted. The status the dollar has enjoyed in this regard has conferred a large degree of power and freedom of action on the US government, an "exorbitant privilege".

References

Adams, F. C. (1971). The Road to Pearl Harbor: A Re-examination of American Far Eastern Policy, July 1937-December 1938. *The Journal of American History* 58(1), 73-92.

Aizhu, C. (2014). Russia, China Agree to Settle More Trade in Yuan and Rouble, *Reuters*, September 9. Retrieved from http://www.reuters.com/article/us-china-russia-idUSKBN0H40X020140909

Al-Ahmed, A., Bond, A., & Morillo, D. (2013). *Security Threats to Saudi Arabia's Oil Infrastructure*, The Institute for Gulf Affairs, Washington D.C. Retrieved from http://www.gulfinstitute.org/wp-content/uploads/2013/11/Threats_to_the_Saudi_Oil_Infrastructure.pdf

Andrews, D.M. (2006). *International monetary power*. Ithaca: Cornell University Press.

Arnold, M. (2016). Europe's Banks Begin Tentative Return to Iran. *Financial Times*, April 3. Retrieved from http://www.ft.com/cms/s/0/75dc8d7e-f830-11e5-803c-d27c7117d132.html#axzz4A6SVEGwe

Auzanneau, M. (2018). *Oil, Power, and War: A Dark History*. White River Junction, Vermont: Chelsea Green Publishing.

Beeson, M. (2004). The Rise of the "Neocons" and the Evolution of American Foreign Policy. Paper presented at the Workshop on The Post-Cold War International Order and Domestic Conflict in Asia, National University of Singapore, 29-30

July, 2004. Retrieved from https://espace.library.uq.edu.au/view/UQ:10403

Blanchard, C. M. (2009). Saudi Arabia: Background and U.S. Relations. *Congressional Research Service Report for Congress*. Washington D.C.: Congressional Research Service.

Block, F. L. (1977). *The Origins of International Economic Disorder: A Study of United States International Monetary Policy from World War II to the Present*. Berkeley: University of California Press.

Blum, J. M. (1959). *From the Morgenthau Diaries*. Boston: Houghton Mifflin.

Bordo, M. D. (1993). The Bretton Woods International Monetary System: A Historical Overview. In M. D. Bordo & B. Eichengreen (Eds.), *A Retrospective on the Bretton Woods System: Lessons for International Monetary Reform* (pp. 3-108). Chicago: University of Chicago Press.

Bordo, M. D., Simard, D. & White, E. (1995). France and the Bretton Woods International Monetary System 1960 to 1968. In J. Reis (Ed.), *International Monetary Systems in Historical Perspective* (pp. 153-180). London: Palgrave Macmillan.

Borg, D. (1957). Notes on Roosevelt's "Quarantine" Speech. *Political Science Quarterly, 72*(3), 405-433. doi:10.2307/2145326.

Boughton, J. (2001). Northwest of Suez: The 1956 Crisis and the IMF. *IMF Staff Papers, 48*(3), 425-446.

Broadberry, S. (1998). How Did the United States and Germany Overtake Britain? A Sectoral Analysis of Comparative Productivity Levels, 1870-1990. *The Journal of Economic History, 58*(2), 375-407.

Brugier, C. (2014). China's way: the new Silk Road. *European Union Institute for Security Studies*. Retrieved from https://

www.iss.europa.eu/sites/default/files/EUISSFiles/Brief_14_New_Silk_Road.pdf

Brzezinski, Z. (1998). *The Grand Chessboard: American Primacy and its Geostrategic Imperatives*. New York: Basic Books.

Callinicos, A. (2009). *Imperialism and Global Political Economy*. Cambridge: Polity Press.

Centeno, M. A. & Cohen, J. N. (2012). The arc of neoliberalism. *Annual Review of Sociology*, 38(1), 317-340.

Chinn, M. & Frankel, J. A. (2007). Will the Euro Eventually Surpass the Dollar as Leading International Reserve Currency?In R. H. Clarida (Ed.), *G7 Current Account Imbalances: Sustainability and Adjustment* (pp. 283-338). Chicago: University of Chicago Press.

Chomsky, N. (2003). *Hegemony or Survival: America's Quest for Global Dominance*. New York: Metropolitan Books.

Choucri, N. (1980). OPEC: Calming a Nervous World Oil Market. *Technology Review*, 83(1), 36-45.

Clark, W. R. (2005). *Petrodollar Warfare: Oil, Iraq and the Future of the Dollar*. Gabriola Island, Canada: New Society Publishers.

Cohen, A., Curtis, L., & Graham, O. (2008). The Proposed Iran-Pakistan-India Gas Pipeline: An Unacceptable Risk to Regional Security. *The Heritage Foundation*, Washington D.C., May 30. Retrieved from https://www.heritage.org/asia/report/the-proposed-iran-pakistan-india-gas-pipeline-unacceptable-risk-regional-security

Cohen, B. J. (2011). *The Future of Global Currency: the Euro versus the Dollar*. London: Routledge.

Collins, D. (2013). Rise of the Petro Yuan. *Financial Sense*. April 15. Retrieved from http://www.financialsense.com/contributors/dan-collins/rise-petro-yuan

Cooper, C. L. (1978). *The Lion's Last Roar: Suez, 1956.* New York: Harper & Row.

D'Arista, J. (2009). The evolving international monetary system. *Cambridge Journal of Economics*, 33(4), 633–652.

de Haas, M. (Ed.). (2007). *The Shanghai Cooperation Organisation: Towards a full-grown security alliance?*Clingendael: Netherlands Institute of International Relations. Retrieved from https://www.clingendael.org/sites/default/files/pdfs/20071100_cscp_security_paper_3.pdf

de Haas, M. (2013). *Russian-Chinese Security Relations: Moscow's Threat from the East?*Clingendael: Netherlands Institute of International Relations. Retrieved from https://www.clingendael.org/sites/default/files/pdfs/20130327_rc_securityrelations.pdf

de Haas, M. (2015). The Collective Security Treaty Organization: On its way to a "NATO of the East"? *Central Asia Policy Brief No.26.* Retrieved from https://centralasiaprogram.org/archives/8322

Desai, P. (2005). Russian Retrospectives on Reforms from Yeltsin to Putin. *Journal of Economic Perspectives*, *19*(1), 87–106. doi: 10.1257/0895330053147903

Domhoff, G. W. (2014). The Council on Foreign Relations and the Grand Area: Case Studies on the origins of the IMF and the Vietnam War. *Class, Race and Corporate Power*, *2*(1). doi: 10.25148/CRCP.2.1.16092111

Doran, C. (2012) Iran and the Petrodollar Threat to US Empire. *New Left Project*. August 8. Retrieved from http://www.newleftproject.org/index.php/site/article_comments/iran_and_the_petrodollar_threat_to_u.s._empire

D. P. E. (1945). Lend-Lease: Its Origin and Development: Part I. *Bulletin of International News, 22*(2), 55-62. Retrieved from http://www.jstor.org/stable/25643751

Eichengreen, B. (2009). The Dollar Dilemma: The World's Top Currency Faces Competition. *Foreign Affairs, 88*(5), 53-68.

Eichengreen, B. (2011). *Exorbitant Privilege: The Rise and Fall of the Dollar and the Future of the International Monetary System*. New York: Oxford University Press.

Eichengreen, B. & Flandreau, M. (2012). The Federal Reserve, the Bank of England, and the Rise of the Dollar as an International Currency, 1914–1939. *Open Economies Review* 23(1), 57-87.

Elwell, C. K. (2012). Brief History of the Gold Standard in the United States. *Journal of Current Issues in Finance, Business and Economics, 5*(3), 223-238.

Engdahl. W. (2004a). *A Century of War: Anglo-American Oil Politics and the New World Order*. London: Pluto Press.

Engdahl, F. W. (2004b). A New American Century? Iraq and the Hidden Euro-Dollar Wars. *Global Research*, February 9. Retrieved from http://www.globalresearch.ca/articles/ENG401A.html

Engdahl, F. W. (2011). *Gods of Money: Wall Street and the Death of the American Century*. (2nd ed.). Joshua Tree, California: Progressive Press.

Engdahl, F. W. (2016). Russia Breaking Wall St Oil Price Monopoly. *New Eastern Outlook*, January 9. Retrieved from https://journal-neo.org/2016/01/09/russia-breaking-wall-st-oil-price-monopoly/

Fawcett, L. (Ed.). (2013). *International relations of the Middle East* (3rd ed.). Oxford: Oxford University Press.

Fields, D. &Vernengo, M. (2013). Hegemonic currencies during the crisis: The dollar versus the euro in a Cartalist perspective, *Review of International Political Economy*, 20(4), 740-759. doi: 10.1080/09692290.2012.698997

Fourcade-Gourinchas, M. & Babb, S. L. (2002). The Rebirth of the Liberal Creed: Paths to Neoliberalism in Four Countries. *American Journal of Sociology*, 108(3), 533-579.

Fukuyama, F. (1989). The End of History? *The National Interest*, 16, 3-18.

Gavin, F. J. (2002). The Gold Battles within the Cold War: American Monetary Policy and the Defense of Europe, 1960–1963. *Diplomatic History*, 26(1), 61-94. doi:10.1111/1467-7709.00300

Gavin, F. J. (2004).*Gold, Dollars, and Power: The Politics of International Monetary Relations, 1958-1971*. Chapel Hill: University of North Carolina Press Books.

Gillespie, P. (2016). China leads global US debt dump. *CNN*, February 17. Retrieved from https://money.cnn.com/2016/02/17/news/economy/china-us-debt-dump-central-banks/

Goh, E. (2005). Nixon, Kissinger, and the "Soviet Card" in the U.S. Opening to China, 1971–1974. *Diplomatic History*, 29, 475-502. doi:10.1111/j.1467-7709.2005.00500.x

Gokay, B. (2015). Two Pillars of US Global Hegemony: Middle Eastern Oil and the Petrodollar. In I. Ness & Z. Cope (Eds.). *The Palgrave Encyclopedia of Imperialism and Anti-Imperialism*. Palgrave Macmillan.

Gökay, B. & Whitman, D. (2004). Ghost Dance: The U.S. and Illusions of Power in the 21st Century. *Alternatives: Turkish Journal of International Relations*, 3(4), 60-91.

Golan, M. (1976). *The Secret Conversations of Henry Kissinger: Step-By-Step Diplomacy in the Middle East*. New York: Quadrangle.

Gourinchas, P. (2010). U.S. Monetary Policy, 'Imbalances' and the Financial Crisis.Remarks prepared for the Financial Crisis Inquiry Commission Forum, WashingtonDC. February 26-

27. Retrieved from http://economics-files.pomona.edu/colloquium/gourinchas.pdf

Groen, E. (1952). The Significance of the Marshall Plan for the Petroleum Industry in Europe: Historical Review of the Period 1947-1950. In US Congress, *Report on the Third World Petroleum Congress*, Washington D.C: US Government Printing Office.

Grose, P. (1996). *Continuing the Inquiry: the Council on Foreign Relations from 1921 to 1996*. New York: Council on Foreign Relations Press.

Harper, J. L. (1994). *American Visions of Europe—Franklin D. Roosevelt, George F. Kennan and Dean G. Acheson*, Cambridge: Cambridge University Press.

Harvey, D. (2005). *A Brief History of Neoliberalism*. Oxford: Oxford University Press.

Hayes, M. (2008).*The Economics of Keynes: A new guide to the General Theory*. Cheltenham: Edward Elgar Publishing.

Heilmann, S., Rudolf, M., Huotari, M. & Buckow, J. (2014). China's Shadow Foreign Policy: Parallel Structures Challenge the Established International Order. *China Monitor,* 18, October 28. Retrieved from https://www.merics.org/sites/default/files/2018-01/China_Monitor_18_Shadow_Foreign_Policy_EN.pdf

Heiss, M. (1994). The United States, Great Britain, and the Creation of the Iranian Oil Consortium, 1953-1954. *The International History Review, 16*(3), 511-535.

Helleiner, E. (2003). Dollarization diplomacy: US policy towards Latin America coming full circle? *Review of International Political Economy*, 10(3), 406-429, doi: 10.1080/09692290308424

Helleiner, E. (2008). Political Determinants of International Currencies: What Future for the US Dollar? *Review of*

International Political Economy, 15(3), pp. 354-378.

Hera, R. (2012). The war at the end of the dollar. April 12. Retrieved from https://www.mining.com/the-war-at-the-end-of-the-dollar/

Hewitt, A. (2014). China's Gold Market: Progress & Prospects. *Alchemist,* 74. Retrieved from: http://www.lbma.org.uk/assets/blog/alchemist_articles/Alch74Hewitt.pdf

Higgs, R. (2005). Government and the Economy: The World Wars. *Independent Institute Working Paper Number 59*, April 20. Oakland: The Independent Institute. Retrieved from http://www.independent.org/pdf/working_papers/59_government.pdf

Hindy, L. (2017). A Rising China Eyes the Middle East. *The Century Foundation*, April 6. Retrieved from https://tcf.org/content/report/rising-china-eyes-middle-east/

Hinnebusch, R. A. &Ehteshami, A. (eds.). (2002). *The Foreign Policies of Middle East States*. Boulder: Lynne Rienner Publishers.

Horton, S. (n.d.). 'The 1973 Oil Crisis'. Retrieved from https://www.envirothonpa.org/documents/The1973OilCrisis.pdf

Hossein-Zadeh, I. (2006). *The Political Economy of U.S. Militarism.* New York: Palgrave Macmillan.

Hubner, K. (2007). Euro-Dollar Puzzles. In J. Roy & P. Gomis-Porqueras (Eds.), *TheEuro and the Dollar in a Globalized Economy*. Burlington: Ashgate Publishing.

Hudson, M. (1996). To Play the Hegemon: Fifty Years of US Policy toward the Middle East. *Middle East Journal, 50*(3), 329-343.

Hudson, M. (2003). *Super Imperialism: The Origin and Fundamentals of U.S. World Dominance.* London: Pluto Press.

Hudson, M. (2005). *Global Fracture: The New International Economic Order*. London: Pluto Press.

Ilie, L. (2006). Economic considerations regarding the first oil shock, 1973-1974. MPRA Paper No. 6431. St. Louis: Federal Reserve Bank of St Louis. Retrieved from https://mpra.ub.uni-muenchen.de/6431/1/MPRA_paper_6431.pdf

International Monetary Fund. (n.d.). The System in Crisis, 1959-1971. Money Matters: An IMF Exhibit – The Importance of Global Cooperation. Retrieved from https://www.imf.org/external/np/exr/center/mm/eng/mm_sc_03.htm

Jacob, S. (2013). India pushing Iran to Accept Rs for Oil Imports. *Rediff Business*, October 1. Retrieved from http://www.rediff.com/business/report/india-pushing-iran-to-accept-rs-for-oil-imports/20131001.htm

Javaid, U., & Rashid, A. (2015). Oil and Gas Potentials of Central Asian Republics and Relations with Pakistan. *South Asian Studies, 30*(1), 127-148.

Johnson, J. (2008). Forbidden fruit: Russia's uneasy relationship with the US dollar, *Review of International Political Economy*, 15(3), 379-398. doi: 10.1080/09692290801928749

Keohane, R. (2005). *After Hegemony: Cooperation and Discord in the World Political Economy*. Princeton: Princeton University Press.

Khalilzad, Z., Shlapak, D. A. &Byman, D. (1997). *The Implications of the Possible End of the Arab-Israeli Conflict for Gulf Security*. Santa Monica: RAND Corporation. Retrieved from https://www.rand.org/pubs/monograph_reports/MR822.html.

Kingseed, C. C. (1995). *Eisenhower and the Suez Crisis of 1956*. Baton Rouge: Louisiana State University Press.

Kirshner, J. (2008). Dollar Primacy and American Power: What's at Stake? *Review of International Political Economy*, 15(3),

418–438.

Koenig, P. (2016). The Collapse Of The Western Fiat Monetary System May Have Begun. *Information Clearing House*. April 24. Retrieved from http://www.informationclearinghouse.info/article44524.htm

Krauthammer, C. (1991). The Unipolar Moment. *Foreign Affairs* 70(1), 23-33.

Krauthammer, C. (2002). The Unipolar Moment Revisited. *The National Interest*, 70, 5-17.

Krueger, R. (1975). *The United States and International Oil: A report for the Federal Energy Administration on U.S. firms and Government policy*. New York: Praeger.

Kultgen, D. B. (2014). Saudi Aramco: a look ahead, *The Journal of World Energy Law & Business*, 7(2), 153–161. https://doi-org.ezproxy.uws.edu.au/10.1093/jwelb/jwu003

Lahav, P. (2015). The Suez Crisis of 1956 and Its Aftermath: A Comparative Study of Constitutions, Use of Force, Diplomacy and International Relations. *Boston University Law Review*, 95(4), 1297–1354.

Lake, D. A. (2000). British and American Hegemony compared: Lessons for the Current Era of Decline. In J. A. Frieden & D. A. Lake (Eds.), *International Political Economy Perspectives on Global Power and Wealth,*(4th ed.). New York: Routledge. https://doi.org/10.4324/9780203518588

Layne, C. (2009). The Waning of U.S. Hegemony—Myth or Reality?: A Review Essay. *International Security* 34(1), 147-172.

'Lend-Lease and Military Aid to the Allies in the Early Years of World War II'. (n.d.). The Office of the Historian, United States Department of State. Retrieved from https://history.state.gov/milestones/1937-1945/lend-lease

Lerner, G. (2017). In Turkey, US Loss is China's Gain. *The Diplomat*, January 31. Retrieved from https://thediplomat. com/2017/01/in-turkey-us-loss-is-chinas-gain/

Louis, R.W. & Roger, O. (1989). *Suez 1956: The Crisis and its Consequences*. Oxford: Clarendon Press.

Luce, H.R. (1999). The American Century. *Diplomatic History*, 23(2), 159-171.

Luciani, G. (2016). Oil and Political Economy in the International Relations of the Middle East. In L. Fawcett (Ed.), *International Relations of the Middle East*, (4th ed.). (pp. 105-130). Oxford: Oxford University Press.

Lynch, A. C. (2007).The Putin Succession and Russian Foreign Policy, *The Brown Journal of World Affairs*,14(1), 53-64.

Mabro, R. (2008). On the security of oil supplies, oil weapons, oil nationalism and all that. *OPEC Energy Review*, 32, 1-12. doi:10.1111/j.1753-0237.2008.00139.x

Marti, M. E. (2002). *China and the Legacy of Deng Xiaoping: From Communist Revolution to Capitalist Evolution*. Washington D.C.: Potomac Books.

Mastanduno, M. (2009). System maker and privilege taker. *World Politics, 61*(1), 121-154.

McNally, D. (2011). *Global Slump: The Economics and Politics of Crisis and Resistance*. Oakland: PM Press.

Milan, M. (2012). The Financial Crisis and the Dollar Hegemony. *Austral: Brazilian Journal of Strategy & International Relations,* 1(1), 125-140. doi: https://doi.org/10.22456/2238-6912.27996

Mitchell, L. E. (2008). *The Speculation Economy: How Finance Triumphed Over Industry*. San Francisco: Berrett-Koehler Publishers.

Mitchell, T. (2002). McJihad: Islam in the U.S. Global Order. *Social*

Text 20(4), 1-18.

Momani, B. (n.d.). GCC Oil Exporters and the Future of the Dollar. Retrieved from http://www.arts.uwaterloo.ca/~bmomani/Documents/NPE_GCC_Oil_Exporters.pdf

Momani, B. (2008). Gulf Cooperation Council Oil Exporters and the Future of the Dollar. *New Political Economy*, 13(3), 293-314.

Murphy, M. & Yuan, W. J. (2009). Is China Ready to Challenge the Dollar? Internationalization of the Renminbi and its Implications for the United States. *Report of the CSIS Freeman Chair in China Studies*. Washington D.C.: Centre for Strategic Studies and International Studies. Retrieved from https://www.voltairenet.org/IMG/pdf/Is_China_Ready_to_Challenge_the_Dollar_.pdf

National Intelligence Council. (2008). *Global Trends 2025: A Transformed World*. Washington D.C.: US Government Printing Office. Retrieved from https://www.files.ethz.ch/isn/94769/2008_11_Global_Trends_2025.pdf

National Intelligence Council. (2012). *Global Trends 2030: Alternative Worlds*. Washington D.C.: US Government Printing Office. Retrieved from https://globaltrends2030.files.wordpress.com/2012/11/global-trends-2030-november2012.pdf

Newton, C.C.S. (1984). The Sterling Crisis of 1947 and the British Response to the Marshall Plan. *Economic History Review*, 37(3), 391-408.

Nissanke, M. (2009). The Global Financial Crisis and the Developing World: Transmission channels and fall-outs for industrial development. Research and Statistics Branch Working Paper 06/2009, United Nations Industrial Development Organization. Retrieved from https://open.unido.org/

Nkomo, J. C. (2017). Crude Oil Price Hikes and Issues for Energy

Security for Southern Africa.*Journal of Energy in Southern Africa*, 21(2), 12-16. doi: 10.17159/2413-3051/2010/v21i2a3251

Noeth, B. J. & Sengupta, R. (2012). Global European banks and the financial crisis. *Federal Reserve Bank of St. Louis Review*, November/December 2012, 94(6), 457-79. Retrieved from https://files.stlouisfed.org/files/htdocs/publications/review/12/11/Noeth.pdf

Notter, H. A. (1949). *Postwar Foreign Policy Preparation, 1939-1945*. Westport: Greenwood Press.

Ocampo J. A. (2014). The Latin American Debt Crisis in Historical Perspective. In J. E. Stiglitz & D. Heymann (Eds.), *Life After Debt* (pp. 87-115). London: Palgrave Macmillan.

Odell, P. R. (1981). *Oil and World Power: Background to the Oil Crisis*. (6th ed.). Harmondsworth: Penguin.

Office of the Secretary of Defense. (2017). *Annual Report to Congress: Military and Security Developments Involving the People's Republic of China 2017*. Retrieved from https://dod.defense.gov/Portals/1/Documents/pubs/2017_China_Military_Power_Report.PDF

Offner, A. (1977). Appeasement Revisited: The United States, Great Britain, and Germany, 1933-1940. *The Journal of American History, 64*(2), 373-393. doi:10.2307/1901830.

Oksenberg, M. & Economy, E. (Eds.). (1999). *China Joins the World: Progress and Prospects*. New York: Council on Foreign Relations Press.

Oliver, R. W. (1984). Bretton Woods: a retrospective essay. *Humanities Working Paper 108*. Pasadena: California Institute of Technology. Retrieved from http://resolver.caltech.edu/CaltechAUTHORS:20100629-141604373

O'Neill, J. (2001). Building Better Global Economic BRICs. *Goldman SachsGlobal Economics Paper No. 66*. Retrieved from https://www.goldmansachs.com/insights/archive/archive-pdfs/build-better-brics.pdf

O'Sullivan, C. (1999). Sumner Welles, Postwar Planning and the Quest for a New World Order, 1937-1943. Dissertation: London School of Economics. ProQuest Dissertations & Theses.

Painter, D. S. (1984). Oil and the Marshall Plan. *Business History Review*,58(3), 359-383.

Painter, D. S. (1993).*The United States, Great Britain, and Mossadegh*. Pew Case Studies in International Affairs. Institute for the Study of Diplomacy, Georgetown University.

Panitch, L., &Gindin, S. (2012). *The Making of Global Capitalism: The Political Economy of American Empire*. London: Verso.

Panko, R. (2016). Goodbye Petrodollar: Russia Accepts Yuan, Is Now China's Biggest Oil Partner. *Russia Insider*. February 3. Retrieved from http://russia-insider.com/en/politics/saudi-arabia-has-lost-asia-russia-now-chinas-biggest-oil-partner/ri12611

Parker, R., &Whaples, R. (2013). *Routledge handbook of major events in economic history*. New York: Routledge.

Prasad, E. S. (2014). *The Dollar Trap: How the U.S. Dollar Tightened Its Grip on Global Finance*. Princeton: Princeton University Press.

Putz, C. (2016). India and Pakistan to Join SCO, Is Iran Next? *The Diplomat*. May 26. Retrieved from http://thediplomat.com/2016/05/india-and-pakistan-to-join-sco-is-iran-next/

Reinsch, P. S. (1902). *Colonial Government: An Introduction to the Study of Colonial Institutions*. New York: Macmillan.

Richman, S. L. (1988). The Reagan Record on Trade: Rhetoric vs. Reality. *Cato Institute Policy Analysis No. 107*. Retrieved from https://www.cato.org/publications/policy-analysis/

reagan-record-trade-rhetoric-vs-reality

Rickards, J. (2011). *Currency Wars: The Making of the Next Global Crisis. New York:* Portfolio/Penguin.

Roberts, P. C. (2007) Impending Destruction of the US Economy. *Countercurrents*, November 29. Retrieved from http://www.countercurrents.org/roberts291107.htm

Roberts, P. C. (2013a). The Dying Dollar. *Paul Craig Roberts: Institute for Political Economy.* November 22. Retrieved from http://www.paulcraigroberts.org/2013/11/22/dying-dollar-paul-craig-roberts/

Roberts, P. C. (2013b). Washington Signals Dollar Deep Concerns. *Paul Craig Roberts: Institute for Political Economy*, May 18. Retrieved from http://www.paulcraigroberts.org/2013/05/18/washington-signals-dollar-deep-concerns-paul-craig-roberts/

Robinson, W. I. (1996). *Promoting Polyarchy: Globalization, US Intervention, and Hegemony.* Cambridge: Cambridge University Press.

Rofe, J. S. (2007). *Franklin Roosevelt's Foreign Policy and the Welles Mission.* Palgrave Macmillan. doi: 10.1057/9780230604896.

Rofe, J. S. (2012). Pre-war Post-war Planning: The Phoney War, the Roosevelt Administration, and the Case of the Advisory Committee on Problems of Foreign Relations. *Diplomacy & Statecraft, 23*(2), 254-279.

Roots, R. I. (2000). Government by permanent emergency: The forgotten history of the new deal constitution. *Suffolk University Law Review, 33(2),* 259-292.

Rosenberg, E. (1985). Foundations of United States International Financial Power: Gold Standard Diplomacy, 1900–1905. *Business History Review,* 59(2), 169-202.

Rosenman, S. I. (1952). *Working with Roosevelt.* New York: Harper.

Rumer, E., Sokolsky, R. &Stronski, P. (2016). *US Policy Toward Central Asia 3.0.* Carnegie Endowment for International Peace. Retrieved from https://carnegieendowment. org/2016/01/25/u.s.-policy-toward-central-asia-3.0-pub-62556

Schiff, P. (2015). Currencies Depend on Faith, Gold Doesn't. *SchiffGold*, July 24. Retrieved from https://schiffgold.com/ commentaries/currencies-depend-on-faith-gold-doesnt/

Schmitz, D. (1999). *Thank God They're on Our Side; the United States and Right-wing Dictatorships, 1921-1965.* Chapel Hill: University of North Carolina Press.

'Secretary of State John Hay and the Open Door in China, 1899–1900'. (n.d.). The Office of the Historian, United States Department of State. Retrieved from https://history.state. gov/milestones/1899-1913/hay-and-china

Shoup, L. H. (1975). Shaping the Postwar World: The Council on Foreign Relations and United States War Aims During World War II.*The Insurgent Sociologist,* 5(3), 7-52. https:// doi.org/10.1177/089692057500500302

Shoup, L. H. (2015). *Wall Street's Think Tank: The Council on Foreign Relations and the Empire of Neoliberal Geopolitics, 1976-2014.* New York: Monthly Review Press.

Shoup, L. H.& Minter, W. (1977). *Imperial Brain Trust: the Council on Foreign Relations and United States Foreign Policy.* New York: Monthly Review Press.

Shoup, L., & Minter, W. (2004). *Imperial Brain Trust: the Council on Foreign Relations and United States Foreign Policy.* Lincoln: Authors Choice Press.

Simha, R.K. (2016). Currency Dictatorship: The Struggle to End US Dollar Hegemony.*Global Research,* January 17.Retrieved from http://www.globalresearch.ca/currency-dictatorship-the-struggle-to-end-us-dollar-hegemony/5501829

Skidelsky, R. (2001). *John Maynard Keynes, Vol. 3: Fighting for Freedom, 1937-1946*. London: Viking-Penguin.

Spiro, D. E. (1999).*The Hidden Hand of American Hegemony: Petrodollar Recycling and International Markets*. Ithaca: Cornell University Press.

Sputnik. (2016). New Silk Road: Iran to Connect Europe, China by Train Route. *Sputnik*, February 15. Retrieved from http://sputniknews.com/business/20160215/1034800797/iran-china-train-silk-road.html

Steger, M., Battersby, P. &Siracusa, J. (Eds.). (2014). *The SAGE Handbook of Globalization*.http://dx.doi.org/10.4135/9781473906020

Steil, B. (2013). *The Battle of Bretton Woods: John Maynard Keynes, Harry Dexter White, and the Making of a New World Order*. Princeton: Princeton University Press.

Steil, B. & Walker, D. (2015). The Spread of Central Bank Currency Swaps Since the Financial Crisis. *Council on Foreign Relations,*April 9. Retrieved from https://www.cfr.org/interactives/central-bank-currency-swaps-since-financial-crisis#!/?cid=from_interactives_listing

Stettinius, E. (1944). *Lend-Lease: Weapon for Victory,* Harmondsworth: Penguin.

Stokes, D. (2014). Achilles' deal: Dollar decline and US grand strategy after the crisis, *Review of International Political Economy*, 21:5, 1071-1094. doi: 10.1080/09692290.2013.779592

Strange, S. (1987). The Persistent Myth of Lost Hegemony. *International Organization, 41*(4), 551-574.

Tétreault, M. A. (2008). The Political Economy of Middle Eastern

Oil. In J. Schwedler & D. J. Gerner (Eds.), *Understanding the Contemporary Middle East*, (3rd ed.). (pp. 255-279). Boulder: Lynne Rienner.

The BRICS Post. (2016).IMF reforms: China, India, Brazil, Russia Get Greater Say. *The BRICS Post*, January 28. Retrieved from http://thebricspost.com/imf-reforms-china-india-brazil-russia-get-greater-say/#.V1Kr8r55JW8

'The Spanish-American War, 1898'. (n.d.). The Office of the Historian, United States Department of State. Retrieved from https://history.state.gov/milestones/1866-1898/spanish-american-war

Thines, S. (2008). From Soviet federalism to the creation of the Commonwealth of Independent States (CIS). CVCE: University of Luxembourg. Retrieved from https://www.cvce.eu/content/publication/2008/9/4/caa796f9-24f0-4e25-98da-4e98b20f18c8/publishable_en.pdf

Trachtenberg, M. (2011). The French Factor in U.S. Foreign Policy during the Nixon-Pompidou Period, 1969–1974. *Journal of Cold War Studies* 13(1), 4-59.

Trachtenberg, M. (2012).*The Cold War and After: History, Theory, and the Logic of International Politics*. Princeton: Princeton University Press.

Triffin. R. (1978). Gold and the Dollar Crisis: Yesterday and Tomorrow.*Essays in International Finance No. 132*, December. Princeton: Princeton University Press. 1978. Retrieved from https://ies.princeton.edu/pdf/E132.pdf

United States Congressional Research Service. (2019). *China's Economic Rise: History, Trends, Challenges, and Implications for the United States*. Report prepared for Members and Committees of Congress. Retrieved from https://fas.org/sgp/crs/row/RL33534.pdf

United States Department of State. (1948). U.S. Objectives with Respect to the USSR to Counter Soviet Threats to U.S.

Security. NSC 20/4. November 23. Washington, D.C.: Government Printing Office. Retrieved from https://www.mtholyoke.edu/acad/intrel/coldwar/nsc20-4.htm

United States General Accounting Office. (1984). U.S. Role as Contracting Agent for the U.S.-Saudi Arabian Joint Commission on Economic Cooperation. Report NSIAD-84-48. May 14. Retrieved from https://www.gao.gov/products/NSIAD-84-48

United States House of Representatives, 77th Congress 1st Session. (1941). *Report No. 18: To Promote The Defense of the United States*. Report submitted to accompany H.R. 1776 (Lend-Lease Act). January 30. Retrieved from http://www.ibiblio.org/pha/policy/1941/1941-01-30a.html.

Venkataramani, M. S. (1960). Oil and Us Foreign Policy During the Suez Crisis 1956-7. *International Studies*, 2(2), 105–52. https://doi.org/10.1177/002088176000200201

Waldau, G. (2015). China launch of renminbi payments system reflects Swift spying concerns. Financial Times, October 8. Retrieved from http://www.ft.com/intl/cms/s/0/84241292-66a1-11e5-a155- 02b6f8af6a62.html#axzz4A6SVEGwe

Wallerstein, I. M. (1991). *Geopolitics and Geoculture: Essays on the Changing World-System*. New York: Cambridge University Press.

Wallerstein, I. (2006). The Curve of American Power. *New Left Review* 40, 77-94.

Welles, B. (1997). *Sumner Welles: FDR's Global Strategist*. New York: Palgrave Macmillan.

Wihtol, R. (2015). Beijing's Challenge to the Global Financial Architecture. *Georgetown Journal of Asian Affairs*, 2(1), retrieved from https://issuu.com/georgetownsfs/docs/gjaa_vol._2_no._1

Wilson, D. &Purushothaman, R. (2003). Dreaming with BRICs:

The Path to 2050. *Goldman SachsGlobal Economics Paper No. 99*. Retrieved from https://www.goldmansachs.com/insights/archive/archive-pdfs/brics-dream.pdf

Xiaochuan, Z. (2009). Reform the International Monetary System. *BIS Review 41/2009*, March 23. Retrieved from https://www.bis.org/review/r090402c.pdf

Yergin, D. (2008).*The Prize: The Epic Quest for Oil, Money & Power*. New York: Free Press.

Yergin, D. (2011).*The Prize: The Epic Quest for Oil, Money & Power*. New York: Simon and Schuster.

Zhang, H. & Li, M. (2013). Sino-Indian Border Disputes. *Analysis*, 181. Retrieved from https://www.ispionline.it/sites/default/files/pubblicazioni/analysis_181_2013.pdf

Zimmerman, T. (2015). *The New Silk Roads: China, the U.S., and the Future of Central Asia*. NYU Centre on International Cooperation, New York University. Retrieved from: https://cic.nyu.edu/sites/default/files/zimmerman_new_silk_road_final_2.pdf

Index